The Approaching Sabbath

SPIRITUAL DISCIPLINES FOR PASTORS

Thomas R. Swears

ABINGDON PRESS
NASHVILLE

THE APPROACHING SABBATH:
SPIRITUAL DISCIPLINES FOR PASTORS

Copyright © 1991 by Abingdon Press

This book is printed on recycled, acid-free paper.

Library of Congress Cataloging-in-Publication Data

SWEARS, THOMAS R., 1946–
    The approaching Sabbath: spiritual disciplines for pastors /
Thomas R. Swears.
    p.   cm.
    Includes bibliographical references.
    ISBN 0-687-01577-4 (alk. paper)
    1. Clergy—Religious life. I. Title.
BV4011.6.S84   1991
248.8'92—dc20   90-26297
                                                            CIP

Scripture quotations are from the New Revised Standard Version of the
Bible, copyright © 1989 by the Division of Christian Education of the
National Council of Churches of Christ in the United States of America,
and are used by permission.

Contents

CONTENTS

Foreword

It is not mine to say who will or who will not be helped by this book. However, I do feel confident in saying that it will be of particular benefit to those ministers whose seminary preparation concentrated on crises in the parish—death, grief, domestic abuse, economic injustices, social turmoil—but who now face the challenge of the routine, the habitual, and those Sundays which come with unrelenting regularity. But whether one faces the approaching Sabbath with aching weariness and dread or with anticipation, there is refreshment in this slender volume. Thomas Swears has chronicled that week-after-week move of the pastor toward Sunday with the realism of one who does it himself, but with the hope and joy of one who has learned the secret of a sufficiency for ministry in plenty and in want. That secret, the author will tell us, is integrity, the centering of life and work, the ability to be doing only one thing while doing many things, the experience of freedom while under heavy obligations.

Tom Swears is under no illusions that this integrity is without price, a given in the very fact of our being ministers. On the contrary, there are factors in ministry that daily, in ways subtle and not so subtle, tear and pull at one's integrity. For example, who among us has not felt keenly the thrust of Paul's stabbing questions in Romans 3:21-23 (in paraphrase): You who lead others in worship, are you worshiping? You who lead the congregation in prayer, are you praying? You who pronounce offertory sentences, are you a generous steward? Or again, have we not worked hard at being "just one of the folk," welcoming every occasion that permits sweatshirt, blue jeans, and a floppy hat, perhaps sprinkling our conversation with a four-letter word or two, only to be reminded by one phone call, one inquiry, one plea, that we are not "just one of the folk"? The call, the theological education, the ordination reappear at the question, Is there any word from God?

Do not misunderstand: The author is serious about ministry but neither heavy-footed nor heavy-faced about it. He reminds rather than chastises. He invites us into the chapel for prayer, into the family circle, out among the parishioners, into the study, and before the Sunday assembly. Those who accept the invitation will find themselves entering, or re-entering, that life which is both duty and delight.

Fred B. Craddock
Candler School of Theology
Emory University

Preface

A minister of Christ should have his tongue, his heart, and his hand agree.

—JEROME

Every minister who has the continuing responsibility of leading corporate worship on Sunday morning appreciates the meaning of what is conveyed by the title of this book, that is, the approaching sabbath. Some greet it with enthusiasm, freshness, and joy. Others greet it with spent energy, dryness, and a sense of dread. Nevertheless, it approaches every seventh day for every minister whether or not the minister feels ready and prepared for its coming. The purpose of this book is to help those who serve the church as pastors, and will probably do so for years to come, to be better prepared in heart and mind and soul for this work. It is a book about the integrity of the minister's life of study and prayer, which can lead the minister to a more deliberate and focused presence throughout the whole of life.

I wish to acknowledge my gratitude to my post-seminary teacher, Fred Craddock, for the influence of his life upon my own; to my uncle, Glenn O. Blough, for his support and wise counsel; to my wife, Linda, for her love and encouragement; to our three-year-old daughter, Mollie, for the simple joy and energy of her life, which helped keep me properly focused; to my typist and good friend, Judy Miller, for her skill, patience, and ready hand; and to the people of Faith Lutheran Church, Cockeysville, Maryland, and The Lutheran Church of the Good Shepherd, Wilmington, Delaware, who have faithfully and patiently helped me to grow as a pastor and as a person.

Thomas R. Swears
Wilmington, Delaware

CHAPTER ONE

The Spiritual Formation
of the Pastor

We name ourselves by the choices we make.
—MADELEINE L'ENGLE

The life of critical reflection is the process by which one becomes conformed to the image and mind of Christ, thereby living more faithfully and serving more responsively in the world. For the pastor, study and prayer are key elements in this process, because they help direct attention clearly and deliberately into proper channels of spiritual formation.

The process of spiritual formation is not an option some people choose while others do not. It is not a pursuit only for the pious and the deeply committed or those who feel called to it as others might feel called, say, to social action. Rather, the material for spiritual formation is present in every experience of life. As Dag Hammarskjöld observed, at every moment we choose ourselves.[1] In our responses to our experiences and relationships we become shaped into some kind of being. The goal of Christian spiritual formation is to have that being be conformed to the image and mind of Christ. Every experience, every response, every emotion of life provides the material of spiritual formation for every person. The question is not whether we are engaged in spiritual formation. The question is, In what kind of spiritual formation are we engaged? Is the image of Christ or the image of the world being formed in us?[2] Paul, in describing the consecrated life, says, "Do not be conformed to this world, but be transformed by the renewing of your minds, so that you may discern what is the will of God—what is good and acceptable and perfect" (Rom. 12:2). Spiritual formation is deliberate and gradual, although there may be peak moments in it such as Paul himself experienced.

We live in the world and the world provides the material for spiritual formation. Yet we are not to be conformed to the world but to Christ. As Paul says elsewhere in Romans, "Instead, put on the Lord Jesus Christ, and make no provision for the flesh, to gratify its desires" (Rom. 13:14). The goal of Christian spiritual formation is conformity to God's purposes as revealed in Christ. Again Paul says it clearly in II Corinthians 3:18: "And all of us . . . are being transformed into the same image from one degree of glory to another; for this comes from the Lord, the Spirit."

The self-reflective life of study and prayer is an aid to spiritual formation because it helps us more clearly perceive the choices we are making and more deliberately reform them into the image of Christ in and through our lives. We do name ourselves by the choices we make. Each decision, each act, each response for Christ roots us firmly in the image and mind of Christ, and firmly commits us to imitating the likeness of Christ.

The Tasks of the Ordained Ministry

The very act of ordering priorities becomes an act of spiritual formation for the pastor, who has many demands and expectations placed upon his or her time and energy. Various Christian traditions place differing emphases upon the central tasks of the ordained ministry. Among these perceived central tasks in different denominations are Teaching Elder, Chief Elder, Preacher, Sacramental Officer, Confessor, Liturgical Officer, Spiritual Guide, Counselor, Intercessor, Pastor, Administrator, and Healer. Further complicating the ordering of priorities for the pastor are expectations for the tasks of the ordained ministry as defined within any particular congregation. The pastoral ministry clearly is not a one-dimensional task.

The Alban Institute has devised ten models of ordained ministry that attempt to establish more clearly what it is that people expect from their pastor. The study was motivated by the observation that pastors and congregations often get into trouble because of unclarified and unmet expectations in their relationship to each other. The ten models defined in the study are: Counselor-Healer-Caretaker, Minister of the Word, Administrator-Manager of an Organization, Prophet-Social Activist, Social Exemplar, Ring Leader, Community Personage, Celebrant, Spiritual Guide, and Witness.[3] Lyle E. Schaller also has devised a list of pastoral priorities in an attempt to clarify similar questions: What are the priorities on the minister's time as seen by the congregation? What does the minister see as the order of priorities on his or her time? Schaller's list is made up of these several pastoral priorities: Visiting, Teaching, Counseling, Administration, Evangelism, A Leader Among Leaders, Community Leader, The Leader, Personal and Spiritual Growth, Denominational and Ecumenical Responsibilities, Leading Worship and Preaching, and Enabler.[4]

Lists such as these point out the complexity of forming a meaningful response to the question, What is the pastor supposed to do? Given such diversity concerning the central tasks and priorities of the ordained ministry, what guiding focus or organizing principle can or ought to be at the center of a pastor's life helping to order these tasks and priorities in a meaningful, sustainable manner? Throughout this book the underlying premise is that the continuing and contemplated spiritual formation of the pastor can provide such a guiding, organizing, and sustaining focus.

Spiritual Formation and Administration

The most immediate dilemma for many pastors in establishing clear and guiding priorities comes in the perceived conflict between spirituality and administration. Yet, administration properly viewed does not need to stand in opposition to pastoral ministry. Rather, it can be an important, dynamic aspect of it, often serving as a channel of grace if so perceived and acted upon.

In a research study involving interviews with some fifty able administrators, John C. Wagner discovered several important themes connecting spirituality and administration. These themes are: integrity, wholeness, community, purpose, discernment, and compassion. Although the themes are interdependent and mutually reinforce one another, integrity was the central theme the administrators spoke about in the connection between spirituality and administration.[5] Integrity includes reliability, but it is also more than that. As an administrator a pastor can be reliable while at the same time distant, cold, and calculating. Integrity, the coherence of faith and life, includes the capability of calling into question and discipline inhumane practices and harmful dynamics that can be involved in the work of administration. Given the difficult and at times painful decisions which are part of corporate life, it is important for pastors as administrators to be both fair and compassionate. It is important for pastors to maintain an authenticity in their daily routine of administrative tasks that encourages and preserves in the congregation an atmosphere of trust. The pastor is at the heart of a trusting congregation and is called to model trustworthiness to others so that they too may develop more deeply into people of trustworthiness, compassion, and integrity themselves. As one administrator interviewed by Wagner put it, what is needed for good administration is *essere humano*—to be human. To develop and maintain this essential quality requires some contemplation. It is not automatic in even the most compassionate of administrators. In Wagner's study almost every administrator spoke of having some time available in the day for solitude and reflection, which they saw as a necessity. The greater the demands of the work, the clearer is the need for planned quiet time and space to gather the scattered forces of one's own life in the presence of God. *Essere humano* in the life of the pastor as administrator does not mean moral perfection. It means authentic human living grounded in the presence and grace of God and lived out daily in one's relationships and experiences with others.

For the pastor a persistent challenge to maintaining such a centered life is the frequency of unscheduled events and interruptions that is part of nearly every working day. How these are perceived and responded to is a large part of the daily grist of the pastor's mill. A key to integrating them meaningfully and faithfully into one's daily life lies in perceiving them as opportunities for ministry rather than as irritations.

My young daughter and I have devised a way of dealing with such unplanned disruptions in our lives. We know a child's chant, which we sing together to comfort ourselves when it is raining and we cannot go outside. The words to the chant are: "There will be weather whether it's cold or hot. There will be weather, whether or not." There is common sense wisdom in that chant which can be applied to the interruptions that regularly occur in the life of any reasonably accessible pastor. First, such interruptions will happen, like the weather, whether one likes them or not. Second, how one responds to them is the key to their being either constant irritations or regular opportunities for ministry and material for spiritual formation in the customary round of daily life and work.

We do, indeed, choose ourselves in every moment of life, and we name ourselves by the choices we make regarding the ordinary events of any single day. To see and to value the basic material for one's own continuing spiritual formation in such ordinary matters is freeing, helpful, and wise.

Saying No Well and Yes Faithfully

Though such opportunities for ministry are regularly presented, this does not mean that each has to be responded to in the same manner. There is an appropriate place both for yes and for no in the pastor's vocabulary. However, pastors often find it difficult to say no. Yet always saying yes can lead to poor stewardship of time and resources as well as to personal frustration and burnout. "People who go into the ministry today," according to William Willimon and Stanley Hauerwas, "are generally nice people. They want to please and to be liked. So it almost becomes impossible for them to say no. As a result, being a minister today is like being nibbled to death by ducks."[6]

The need to say yes is related to two commonly held standards: people pleasing and perfectionism. Nearly everyone likes to be liked and most people like to do things well, or at least not poorly. Such standards are understandable given today's social pressures, family expectations, and cultural influences, but that doesn't automatically make them appropriate.

Many pastors share a significant problem in common with lay people: Their lives are too complex and overcrowded. They may have good intentions, but often they are too busy to be good spouses, parents, or friends. Yet when they attempt to withdraw from some of the demands placed on them they quickly can begin to feel guilty. Professional status, social obligations, church committees, and membership in civic organizations all put demanding claims on time and energy.

Out of a sense of duty pastors attempt to meet personally perceived minimums of involvement in several areas of obligation but often end up exhausted and resentful. They can begin to feel out of control and fragmented, pulled in many directions at the same time. There is no single center but a multiplicity of centers, each clamoring for recognition and control. No one can do this indefinitely and remain healthy. Pastors making the effort experience inner discontinuity brought on by the overabundance of such claims on their resources and their accompanying inability to say no to those claims. They begin to think of themselves in the way Thomas Kelly once observed of such people: not as a single self, but as a committee of selves.[7] The problem is the lack of integration at the core of being, which results in the fragmenting pull of many obligations and the attempt to fulfill them all. The result is stress on two fronts: (1) The hectic pace of daily outward responsibilities and, (2) an inward scatteredness.

A healthy goal in relation to such stresses is to be able to say no as well as yes with confidence and without guilt. This can be done freely and well only when life is lived from a clearly focused center, which is a principle the Quakers have long understood. They refer to it as possessing a singleness of eye. In using this image they weren't original, having taken their cue from Jesus in the Sermon on the Mount: "If your eye is healthy, your whole body will be full of light" (Matt. 6:22). The problem involved in developing such singleness of eye is that so many things seem important, which is precisely why it is hard to say no to them. So it becomes necessary to look more closely at what stands behind saying yes and saying no.

Whenever a decision either for yes or for no is made on the basis of such calculated considerations as, "What will they think of me if I don't do it?" justification is being sought for a harried and unfree life, one that is bound to the opinions and desires of others. But, when a life is rooted in the presence of Christ, with a single focus, then either yes or no can be spoken, not on the basis of what others will think or out of guilt, but from what the Quakers call an inward rising to encourage or discourage the acceptance of the task. Such a focus provides freedom from having to give any reason at all for saying either yes or no, except one: the will of God as it is honestly discerned in one's own life. A life with such a center can be more simply lived but it is not simplistic. Its worth is no longer determined by gaining the good opinion of others or having met the often severe demands of one's own personal expectations. It is determined, rather, by the gracious presence of God and the singleness of eye cultivated in that presence, which nurtures appropriate discernment and decision making.[8]

Sometimes pastors say yes to things that do not follow the clearest markings of their own inner risings. Following such inner risings will mean saying yes to some tasks and no to others. Learning to say yes or no, responsibly and appropriately, is best guided by following such inner risings, rooted neither in the opinion of others nor in vanity, but in a clearly focused center—the presence of Christ—at the heart of life. Such a center nurtures the capability to do more than understand the meaning of the words yes and no. It also enhances the ability to say them more freely and appropriately in response to the variety of opportunities that present themselves in the life of any conscientious pastor.

Saying yes faithfully begins with saying no well, because such appropriate no's allow the time and energy needed for saying yes to opportunities that are more fitting to respond to in the affirmative. Here are some practical suggestions to consider when deciding whether to say yes or no to a new responsibility or opportunity to serve:

• Saying no to a negative energy drain leaves room for the positive use of that energy in creative and healing ways; for instance, saying no to gossip allows space for speaking a gracious word.

• Yeses should be considered prayerfully and carefully, which was the theme of Jesus' counting the cost parables of the tower builder and of the king going out to battle against an enemy found in Luke 14:28-32. It is important to know what is required.

• Say yes to things that add meaning to life, not simply credentials or more activity. Such false yeses look good and may even open doors. But they are self-deceptions, not honest responses, and there is no health in them.

• The lack of a focused spiritual center makes an appropriate yes difficult. Every opportunity can appear to be either essential or worthless as one drifts from one thing to another, passively hoping for something meaningful to happen.

• When one is properly centered in Christ it is quite possible for there to be more appropriately chosen yeses to sacrificial opportunities than self-serving ones, as Jesus himself taught: "Those who want to save their life will lose it, and those who lose their life for my sake, and for the sake of the gospel, will save it" (Mark 8:35). Not every yes in life needs to be enjoyable. There are times when those that aren't enjoyable at all possess the fullest meaning. This was true, for instance, of Jesus' own clearest and most difficult yes, spoken in the Garden of Gethsemane: "Father, if you are willing, remove this cup from me; yet, not my will but yours be done" (Luke 22:42).

Sometimes yes is appropriate not because it is enjoyable but because it is a responsible act of stewardship and of devotion to Christ. Paul described such an experience when he wrote to the Corinthians, "If I proclaim the gospel, this gives me no ground for boasting, for an obligation is laid on me, and woe to me if I do not proclaim the gospel! For if I do this of my own will, I have a reward; but if not of my own will, I am entrusted with a commission" (I Cor. 9:16-17). Learning to say yes faithfully is as important as learning to say no well. There is a needed place for both in the vocabulary of responsible, committed, and loving pastors.

The Life of Reflection

In describing influences that have helped form his life and ministry, Gardner Taylor, pastor of Concord Baptist Church in Brooklyn, has spoken of a reverenced scholarship in the lives of his teachers during his student days at Oberlin Seminary.[9] That phrase, reverenced scholarship, is an appropriate one to use in describing the kind of life of study and prayer around which the pastor's ministry can be formed. The focus isn't on information alone or on piety alone. It is on an informed piety in the service of the gospel. Both scholarship and the devotional life can help prepare a place of readiness for the work of the ordained ministry. Ideally, the pastor brings depth of heart and of mind to such tasks. The engagement of the mind only can be sterile. The engagement of the heart alone can lack substance. It is the connection between the heart and the mind that leads to integrity and competence in the various tasks of the ordained ministry.

The reflective life is clearly distinguished in several biblical characters. Moses at Horeb, Elijah in the cave of the desert, Paul in Arabia, John on Patmos,

21

and Jesus at Gethsemane all spent time away from people they were yet to serve through their leadership, their writing, or their sacrificial service.

From the experience of these biblical characters, we can learn an important lesson. Reflection often precedes effective ministry. Whatever its outward form might be, its coherence is found in the wedding of the heart and the mind. Pastor and theologian Joseph Sittler has written perceptively of such a view when he states that the principal work of the ordained ministry is reflection. Clergy persons, he says, have a particular responsibility to the discipline of the reflective life so that their witness to the grace and presence of God will be poignant and strong.[10] Such a view is at the center of the pastor's life of study and prayer, helping properly form that life for the service it is yet to offer.

CHAPTER TWO

Spiritual Formation
in the Family

*By themselves abstractions will not travel. They must pass
through the heart to be transmitted.*

—SAUL BELLOW

Holiness in the Family

Given the daily round of the actual events and
range of emotions in most homes, the title of this
section may seem either unrealistic or naively
informed. It is difficult to be a saint in the midst of
one's own family. Perhaps the single most difficult
place to practice and experience the presence of
holiness is among those known the best and loved the
most. This is so because such persons are seen
regularly in their full humanity, which leaves little
opportunity to fill in unknown areas with conjectures
about their wisdom, compassion, and patience. Such
remarks are often reserved for persons not known
nearly as well. It is easier to imagine the gracious
qualities of someone not known because the less
desirable qualities of one's own family members are
as well known as their more desirable qualities.

Such an internal family dynamic was not unknown even in Jesus' family. The New Testament records little about Jesus' relationships within his own family, yet in the few glimpses we are given there is a hint that in his family he experienced at least some of what is experienced in families today. Already by the age of twelve he was a source of worry and irritation for his parents. After he had been missing for three days, his parents found him in the Temple. Mary said to Jesus, "Child, why have you treated us like this? . . . your father and I have been searching for you in great anxiety" (Luke 2:48). Jesus responded, "Why were you searching for me? Did you not know that I must be in my Father's house?" (Luke 2:49). And Luke reports of this incident that Mary and Joseph did not understand Jesus (Luke 2:50). It is not an altogether smoothly flowing adolescence being described here.

On into Jesus' adulthood the expectations and irritations remained. At the marriage at Cana in Galilee, Mary was present with an untested expectation that her son would do something to help when the wine gave out. Jesus' direct response to her was this: "Woman, what concern is that to you and to me? My hour has not yet come" (John 2:4). Although this is a reference to Jesus' approaching death, it does evoke images of other sons and daughters who have felt the urge or have actually spoken similar words to parents who have assumed the interest of their children.

Jesus lived in a real family that experienced disappointment, conflict, and irritation such as is known in many families today where real and persistent difficulties present daily challenges. It would be inaccurate and dishonest to dismiss the conflicts to which families are susceptible. The family can be a place of pathology as well as a place of health.

Nevertheless, in the ordinary routine of family life, with all its vicissitudes, grace does break through to heal and renew hope and deepen the capacity to love. I haven't known a more sacred moment than when our infant daughter was taken off an airplane from Korea and placed in my arms. It was a moment brimming with hope and promise, with vulnerability, the fear of the unknown and the yet to be, the weight of responsibility, and the joy of fulfillment. All this was present in one sacred moment that on the outside looked quite ordinary—a man holding a baby—but for me was a moment of holiness.

For many people, pastors included, marriage and family life are the central and most precious Christian vocation. And it is often in the ordinary experiences of family living that holiness, which is the presence of God breaking into the midst of normal human activity, can most fully be known. Such was true in the case of an elderly woman who was confronted by her great-grandson with the question, "How old are you, Grandma?" "I'm eighty-nine," she replied. Next, with all the guilelessness common to little children, he asked, "Then why aren't you dead yet?" "I guess it's because every time I start to lie down for a rest, someone seems to need a sandwich," was all she answered.[1]

To the sensitive ear and searching heart that exchange was a moment of holy encounter. It was the presence of grace flowing through the ordinary conversation of an old woman and a young boy. Holiness is the second sight that sees mystery in the commonplace and grace in the daily round of

25

activity. If people who live in families don't antici-
pate or experience the presence of the holy in the
ordinary events and relationships of their lives, then
they are routinely missing the most consistent,
regular opportunity they have for doing so.

God chose to do an extraordinary thing through a
common human experience—birth into a family. It
was in the crucible of that ordinary human environment—the family—that the holiness of God entered
human experience concretely. It is still a special
place, where holiness can be encountered concretely
every day. To have an experience of the holy is to
sense the presence of God in that person or event.
Since God has abandoned nothing God created, the
possibility of holy encounter is everywhere present,
and perhaps especially in home and family life.

Need and Remembrance

Nevertheless, often the most awkward and difficult
place for a pastor to maintain a consistent, meaningful model of spiritual formation is in the pastor's own
home. I myself have mixed memories of attempts at
family devotions in my own parents' home. As I
recall, formal attempts at gathering in the living
room and following a denominational manual written for such a purpose were awkward at best and
short-lived. Often my sister and I wouldn't want to be
there and my dad seemed out of place in the role of
surrogate pastor which these formal liturgies placed
him in. I sensed that he felt that way himself.
Whenever he said something like "In the name of the
Father and of the Son and of the Holy Ghost. Amen"
in our own living room, it just didn't seem quite right.
And because it didn't, we never sustained such a
discipline for long. Awkwardness and embarrass-

ment aren't good motivators for sustaining a meaningful family devotional life.

Yet there is a need for modeling and nurturing spiritual life in the pastor's home just as there is in every Christian home. It is important to remember, however, that a pastor is not the pastor in his own home. There he is a father or she is a mother, and, in many instances, a parent. He is "Dad" or she is "Mom," not "Pastor" or "Reverend." The behavior of the pastor in the home is that which is appropriate to a spouse or a parent, not that appropriate to a leader of worship in the sanctuary. It is important to be father or mother as well as pastor. After all, before God put us any other place in the world, God put us in a family. The same is true of children. If love and faith are to grow, they need to be nurtured in the well-tended and fertile soil of a healthy home. It is the place where every member of the family can experience the most integrity between what is said and what is done.

Even though formal family devotions can be awkward and difficult to sustain, many people, nevertheless, do have tender remembrances of attempts at devotional life that were modeled for them in the home of their childhood. Looking at some of these models can offer hints for providing experiences appropriate in our own homes today.

My own clearest memory of such devotional life is overhearing my father pray alone at night. It was an unintentional, but powerful, model of the importance of prayer. We lived in a two-story clapboard house in northern Michigan with an enclosed staircase at the center leading up to the bedrooms. I have a fond memory of sitting on that staircase in my pajamas listening to the whispered tones of my father's prayers coming from his bedroom. When he finished I would hear the floorboards creak as he got off his knees and into his bed. To this day it doesn't seem silly to me for a grown man to kneel in prayer and say, "Now I lay me down to sleep . . ." Because I've heard it before, prayed by someone important to me, it has become important to me.

Such modeling of prayer can have a powerful and lasting effect. Family members do watch and listen. What they see and hear helps mold the values they will carry with them into the world. This doesn't mean they need to be set up to listen to prayers being spoken. There is a lack of integrity in that. It simply means, rather, to be aware that whenever prayers are spoken in their presence, even a common table grace or bedtime prayers, family members are observing and listening and learning. Being aware of this dynamic as a powerful learning tool can help guard against taking it too lightly.

A Model: The Common Table Grace

Perhaps the most commonly shared remembrance of family prayers in childhood is the table grace.[2] Many people, pastors included, can remember and perhaps still use as a table grace the prayer, "Come Lord Jesus be our guest and let thy gifts to us be blessed. Amen." To have prayed such a prayer in childhood does not automatically make its continuing use today silly or inappropriate. There are several reasons for this.

First, often there is a fond remembrance connected with such prayers perhaps not consciously present with each use, yet nonetheless nurturing a continuing sense of connectedness to one's spiritual roots. In all likelihood such prayers were learned from parents, grandparents, or remembered Sunday

school teachers. Retaining such spiritual connectedness is a healthy, appropriate, and often warmly
humbling spiritual exercise.

Second, the actual content of such simple table
graces, when evaluated, is neither simple nor
inappropriate for use by any member of the family.
That it is easily remembered is one of the great
benefits of a prayer such as "Come Lord Jesus," as is
the use of vocabulary accessible to all but the
youngest members of the family. And even they can
close their eyes, fold their hands, bow their heads,
and listen, and thus be involved in several significant
aspects of this family liturgy.

Third, the use of commonly known and frequently
used table graces at home begins to nurture a
connection between one's own family and other
Christian families. This is so because such table
graces are the shared possession of the whole church.
A sense of identity and importance is imparted to
people, and especially children, when they can
participate in such prayers while visiting in a friend's
home or attending church dinners. With this in mind,
it is a good practice when asked to lead the prayer at a
church dinner where children are present, to invite
everyone to join in praying together, "Come Lord
Jesus, be our guest . . ." In so doing faithful prayer
will have been offered, warm memories will have
been evoked in some adults, and a growing sense of
participation, identity, and worth will have been
nurtured in the children.

In these several ways a common table grace serves
many of the same functions in a family or religious
community that folk song does in the culture at large.
Part of the power of each is the power of shared
remembrance. There are many such folk songs in the
American culture that are known, sung, and enjoyed

by people of all ages. And there is a sense in which the church too has its own folk songs. They are those hymns which, though technically not folk tunes, nevertheless still function as folk songs within the perimeters of Christian community. Perhaps the best known of these is "Amazing Grace." Another is "Silent Night," especially when sung at the late night candlelight service on Christmas Eve.

The fact that table graces, like folk songs, help form common points of identity, evoke memories, mold a sense of community, use accessible vocabulary, and are easily remembered, ought to encourage the use of both table graces and hymnic folk songs in parish life and family devotions. Don't worry about the proper theology of such prayers and songs, especially with children. Often that is much more a concern of the pastor than it needs to be. Of course, sound theological understanding is important in the home and in the church. What I am speaking of here is simply a matter of balance, perspective, and common sense.

A child's prayer is the beginning of spiritual awareness, not the culminating product of theological reflection. That will come much later. But it is much more likely to come and to be healthy upon arrival if the bearer of it in his or her early years learned to pray "Come Lord Jesus," and "Now I lay me down to sleep," and to sing "Silent night, holy night" while standing with the family in a darkened sanctuary on a Christmas Eve, holding a candle all by himself. Such are the points of common identity and shared experience that nurture a growing spiritual life. Being able to sing and to pray together are powerful and appropriate means of sowing seeds that bear the promise and possibility of healthy fruit.

If such sharing of simple prayers and hymns seems

unimportant, then try a simple experiment one Sunday at worship. Take a seat near a young child who is just learning the Lord's Prayer and can just about say it without help. Listen to the enthusiasm and pride with which the child speaks. She is becoming part of the family we adults know she has been a part of since baptism. But she hasn't known it or experienced it for herself. Now she is. I believe God excuses such pride in a child. In fact, God may enjoy it a bit.

Once I was standing at the altar near a group of young choristers who were participating in worship that day. When I invited the congregation to join in the Lord's Prayer by saying, "As our Lord has taught us, so now we pray," the first clear, strong "Our Father" rang out in unison from those children, all eager to offer a prayer they knew and had learned among us and in their own homes. The sound of their voices swelled many hearts. Do not dismiss the importance of the prayers and hymns that can be commonly known and shared in the home and in the life of the congregation. Faith that lasts a lifetime was often nurtured, early on, through means such as these.

Other suggestions for table blessings include the singing of the doxology, "Praise God from whom all blessings flow; Praise him, all creatures here below; Praise him above, ye heavenly host; Praise Father, Son, and Holy Ghost," or John Cennick's table blessing, "Be present at our table, Lord; Be here and everywhere adored; Thy creatures bless, and grant that we May feast in paradise with thee." Both of these blessings may be sung to the tune "Old Hundredth." A simple spoken table blessing known in many Christian homes is, "Gracious Lord we truly thank you for the food that we are about to receive, for the nourishment of our bodies, for Christ's sake. Amen."

Approaches to Spiritual Formation in the Family

So far we have made two observations about the development of a devotional life in the pastor's home. The first of these is the difficulty of sustaining such a commitment. The second is that a shared pool of remembered or easily learned resources is available for further development and creative use in the home.

The key to developing and sustaining meaningful family devotional life has two principles in common with developing and sustaining meaningful corporate worship life in the congregation: (1) The resource materials need to be appropriate to the capabilities of the participants who will use them, and (2) the leader needs to know the intended goal of what is being done. Without these principles guiding the process there can be considerable floundering even in the most sincere attempts to nurture family devotional life.

My wife is a music instructor who teaches exploratory music to three- and four-year-olds as well as an infant music program for babies and their parents. Lessons can be learned from observing these participants that can be applied to the development of family devotional life.

In the first instance, three- and four-year-olds don't start out learning musical scales or the names of notes on a score. That isn't a helpful beginning point for the exploration of music. The key to successfully nurturing interest and knowledge and skill in music lies in the appropriateness of the instruction to the level of the child's interests and capabilities. So, for instance, rather than learning the meanings of *allegro* and *largo,* or even listening to examples of fast and slow music, children of three and four themselves walk fast and then slow, run and then crawl. This allows them to experience in their own bodies the difference between fast and slow. After doing a series of such activities, they demonstrate their new learning by coloring in either a turtle or a rabbit on a sheet of paper, showing that they recognize fast and slow. And they have great fun doing it.

As a composer, performer, and conductor, my wife knows the importance of *allegro* and *largo.* But she also knows that the children need to learn such concepts essential to their music education at a level appropriate to their interests and capabilities, if a love of music is to be sustained in them as they grow.

The second principle is related to the first. The leader needs to know the intended goal if the participants are ever to get to the desired destination. In the case of the developmental music program for infants, the process begins with the parent tapping a gentle beat on their baby's head or tummy or rocking it to the rhythm of a lullaby. The process moves on to coloring in turtles and rabbits at ages three and four and from there to knowledgeable and responsive choristers responding correctly and enthusiastically when a choral director says to them, *"allegro* singers!"* Knowing where one is going is a big help in getting there and in enjoying the trip along the way.

These same principles can be applied to the development of meaningful and sustainable family devotions in the pastor's home. Perhaps it isn't so essential to start off a young child's devotional life by memorizing parts of Luther's Small Catechism or Calvin's *Institutes* or even the books of the Bible or the Ten Commandments. Why not, instead, begin where the child is and go from there? Words like eschatology and ecclesiology aren't necessary baggage for a child on the trip. God and love are big enough words even for most adults when one stops to think about it.

A common-sense place to begin is around the dinner table or family room. Have a special place and time for sharing. This approach probably isn't too much different from what many are doing now. It is simply more purposeful and done with more awareness. Ask general but not prying questions, ones that show authentic interest in the lives of family members and give them room to respond. Such questions could include: "What did you do today?" "How was your day?" "What did you enjoy doing today?" "What did you learn?" "Did anything sad or funny happen to you?" "What friends did you play with today?" Some questions are more appropriate for younger family members, others for older ones. The important thing is to express interest and concern for each member of the family and allow permission and time for them to share or not to share depending on their need and circumstance. It is also important to share something of oneself.

The special task becomes relating shared experiences to the Christian faith. This basic principle holds true whether the core group for the devotional time is the nuclear family with children at home, the pastor and spouse when the children have left the home, or the unmarried pastor, who shares some devotional time with friends or associates.

The first guard against preaching in leading the devotional life is awareness. The second is discipline. The third is humor. And the fourth is involvement in the conversation and contribution to the prayers by each person participating. Simply ask the other participants what they want included in the prayer and then include it or ask one of them to do so. If a fifteen-year-old is more concerned to ask that a boy named Jason pay more attention to her than she is about world hunger, let it be. We should color in the turtles and rabbits wherever we are. There will be another day for her, a dawning awareness of a larger world and of weightier matters. It will come soon enough to a child born into the nuclear age. It is more important for her to have acceptance and love modeled for her by Christian parents than that she, at fifteen, exhibit a moral consciousness most of her peers and many of her elders don't yet have either. That doesn't mean she is to be left there altogether, any more than selfishness in a five-year-old should be encouraged. It simply means remembering the principles reflected in the turtle and rabbit lesson and being less harried and lighter in approaching the tasks of spiritual formation in the home.

When the resources are fitting and when the leader knows what the goal is—a sustainable and meaningful relationship with God and with one another for each participant appropriate to their capability for such a relationship—then the function of devotional life is being fulfilled in a healthful and maturing way. The goal ought not to be impressiveness in Bible quoting but active responsiveness to biblical principles like love, peace, reconciliation, justice, faithfulness, and hope, at the level of understanding and capability appropriate for each participant. For a five-year-old this might be a lesson on sharing candy with a friend. For oneself it might be the recollection of God's greatest sharing in Christ. Either of those lessons is, potentially, a resource for further spiritual

35

CHAPTER THREE

The Study of Life
as Spiritual Formation

*If you don't find God in the very next person you meet it is a
waste of time looking for him further.*
— GANDHI

The basic laboratory for the study of life is one's
own experience. It is the thing best known, felt the
most deeply, and cared the most about. How to use
such experience as material for spiritual formation is
the focus of this chapter, which will discuss the study
of life under three headings: Awareness, Observation,
and Journaling. The theme connecting these three
topics is that the disciplines of awareness and
observation can be developed and refined through
journaling.

Awareness

Every moment of life is a holy moment. It is part of
the created order in which God is present and which
God has redeemed. Because no experience in life
occurs outside the presence of the One who created
life, all experience bears the potential for divine
revelation. Becoming aware of God's presence and

this potential is a central task of spiritual formation.

To realize that every moment is graced by the presence of God is to sense the transforming possibility in that moment. Such awareness leads to events and relationships having significance they may not have had before. There simply isn't such a thing as an ordinary person or a routine event when an awareness of the presence of God in that person or event is nurtured. Then all persons and events become encounters with the holy because God is present in them. A conversation with the parish secretary concerning the bulletin, a phone call from a young woman asking about a wedding date, and a meeting of the church property committee are all potential encounters with the holy. Because God has not abandoned any part of creation there is opportunity for revelation, learning, and ministry across the full range of relationships and experiences in daily life.

Spiritual formation is enhanced by attentiveness to God's presence in the ordinary events as well as in the deeply moving experiences of life. Such awareness of the presence of God in the ordinary as well as the extraordinary events of daily living is a long-standing means of divine revelation and education. Brother Lawrence *(The Practice of the Presence of God)*, Thomas a Kempis *(The Imitation of Christ)*, and Dag Hammarskjöld *(Markings)* each knew this to be true. Living each moment with the awareness that it is being lived in the presence of Christ is spiritually demanding. Often such awareness is not sustained. However, Christ does not fail to be present because we fail to live in the presence of Christ. The spiritual challenge is to grow into living in Christ's presence more fully. Ultimately that ability is a gift from the Holy Spirit. However, through the discipline of awareness, a responsive heart and mind can be prepared to receive the gifts that God offers.

An old German pastor once told Martin Niemöller, "I count on the Holy Ghost, but the only time he ever spoke to me in the pulpit he said, 'Heinrich, you're lazy.'"[1] It takes commitment, thought, and energy to cultivate an awareness of life being lived in the presence of Christ. Yet such an awareness can enhance a pastor's capability to be a channel of God's grace through ordinary acts of faithfulness in administration, planning, visitation, counseling, teaching, and preaching ministries.

God has not abandoned creation but remains active in it and present to it. Pastors called out by the church to lead others and to speak to them of the meaning and intention of that presence also have the responsibility to live their own lives faithfully with an awareness that they too are doing so in the presence of God. Out of such depth of awareness emerges a maturity of heart and mind that is able to lead the church with patience, integrity, and grace.

Observation

Observation is not the same thing as "there's a sermon in everything." Such a mindset trivializes human experience and uses the holiness of each moment of life in a manipulative way that violates the sacredness of revelation. In developing a sensitive and disciplined approach to observation, the focus is not on getting up some good sermon material. The focus rather is on living obediently and faithfully in the presence of Christ.

Observation as one of the disciplines of spiritual formation doesn't need to force spiritual meanings on events and people. They are already graced by the holy. The pastor's task is not to create something spiritual out of what is perceived to be mundane. It is rather to see what is already there, to reflect on it clearly, and to integrate it meaningfully into the various aspects of pastoral responsibility, from parish administration to presiding at worship.

To sense the holy in the ordinary and the universal in the particular events of a specific time and place is a central task of the discipline of observation. Observing the movement of the holy in the particular events of one's own life will help keep one from trivializing one's own experiences or those of others. Cultivating a sense of the suffering of creation and of the transcendent power and presence of God to redeem that suffering guards against shallow comment and inappropriate spiritualization.

Annie Dillard's descriptions of the presence of the holy in the natural order in *Holy the Firm* are beautifully, clearly, and simply written examples of the power of observation at work without unnecessary spiritualizing of what is already touched by transcendence. In describing the death of a moth consumed in a candle flame, Dillard connects the order of nature to God's transcendent presence.

> One night a moth flew into the candle, was caught, burnt dry, and held . . . A golden female moth, a biggish one with a two-inch wingspan, flopped into the fire, dropped her abdomen into the wet wax, stuck, flamed, frazzled and fried in a second . . . And then this moth-essence, this spectacular skeleton, began to act as a wick. She kept burning . . . for two hours without changing, without bending or leaning—only glowing within, like a building fire glimpsed through silhouetted walls, like a hollow saint, like a flame-faced virgin gone to God, while I

read by her light, kindled, . . . while night pooled wetly at my feet.[2]

Here, in describing an event many people have perhaps seen but not carefully observed, Dillard raises the experience to a higher plain. Through disciplined observation she glimpses more clearly the imminent presence of the transcendent revealed in the death of a single moth.

The discipline of observation can also be cultivated in human relationships. Lutheran theologian Joseph Sittler recalls how his older brother once took their mother, who was from a little town in Ohio, to the Ziegfeld Follies in Chicago. He thought she would be taken aback to see on stage a great 12-foot frame shaped to resemble a book, from which, as the door opened, scantily clad women came out one by one. But she took it all in stride and said only, "Thank you very much. I enjoyed the show." The next spring, when the children of her parish school had a program, she had the local carpenter build a big book, and out of it came little girls, each dressed like one of the women of the Bible. Her power of observation, coupled with faith and imagination, led to a creative application of her experience for the benefit of others.[3] Observation is a faithful, attentive, and responsive way to live in the world. It can deepen one's own experience of the presence of God in each moment of life. And it can nurture openness and sensitivity to others and identity with them in the giving of pastoral care in either its individual or its corporate forms.

Journaling

America's best-known journal is likely Anne Morrow Lindbergh's *Gift from the Sea*. She said of it that she began to write for herself, in order to think out her own individual balance of life, work, and human relationships. And since she thought best with a pencil in hand, she began to write things down. She knew that the process of placing her thoughts and experiences on paper would help her put her life in perspective.[4]

Such perspective on one's own life experiences and relationships is a basic goal of journaling as a discipline of spiritual formation. Journaling becomes a spiritual discipline when it is used to deepen relationships with others and to strengthen faith in God. It can be an important tool in spiritual formation because it leads to further self-revelation and to further revelation of the presence of God in daily life.

None of this growth occurs automatically. Journaling provides a means of reflection and integration only if what is experienced and thought about is written down. Such writing performs two functions. First, the act of writing is in itself clarifying and at times therapeutic. Second, having committed the experience or thought to paper makes it available for further reflection in the future. This section will deal with three issues related to journal writing: (1) Why write it down? (2) What to write down? and (3) How to write it down.

Why Write It Down?

Human memory is fragile and fascinating. Anyone who has tried to get from the shower to the desk without forgetting an idea knows that statement is true. It amazes me that I can remember the score of a basketball game I played in thirty years ago but cannot recall the title of a book I recently read. Much material potentially helpful in personal spiritual formation simply is lost because not enough of it can be recalled to make it useful for reflection and growth. Also a loss to the community of faith are experiences and ideas important to the pastor but not available to the community because the pastor cannot recall them well enough to share them in a meaningful way. It is important to write down impressions of significant experiences, flashes of insight, and subtle urgings if they are to be available as resources either for continuing personal spiritual growth or for the spiritual growth of others. Such experiences and reflection upon them form the substance of spiritual insight into the continuing revelation of God in the world and in one's own life.

A key element of a pastor's spiritual formation is purposeful self-reflection, that is, the development of awareness and a record of the movement of grace in the pastor's own life. To make such use of the material of one's own life is also to make that life available to others as a channel of grace. To capture those often elusive experiences and thoughts in a tangible, usable form, requires discipline and a method for writing them down and recalling them. It is to that task we now turn our attention.

What to Write Down?

This question addresses a practical problem that logically follows a previously stated theological affirmation: All things in life are worthy of note because God created them. However, pastors have neither the time nor the capability nor likely the inclination to make actual note of every experience. Therefore, what to write down is both a theological and a practical concern.

Ernest Campbell, who is a celebrated notetaker himself, provides practical guidance in a story from his own life. He tells how, in the early years of his ministry and with little money, he was visited by a salesman selling plots in the local cemetery of a community where Campbell wasn't intending to stay very long. During the course of their conversation, which took place in Campbell's sparsely appointed living room, the salesman gave a series of what seemed to be nearly prepackaged responses to anticipated excuses for not buying such a plot, most of which Campbell offered. Finally, when he began to stumble in his responses to questions he hadn't anticipated, the salesman simply said, "It's better to have it and not need it than to need it and not have it!"[5]

That practical principle is a helpful starting point in deciding what to write down and what to let go. It is better to have it and not need it than to need it and not have it. If an image or thought is needed, but not available, it cannot be used. If it is available, but not needed, it can always be retrieved for use another time. That cannot be said about something vaguely remembered but now no longer clothed in vivid images of actual life experience.

The common occurrences of life that seem to be touched by the holy are a more specific thing to write down. Often such images are elusive and fragile and easily lost. Yet they are, however delicately so, remnants of the sense the Psalmist enjoyed of how the heavens declare the glory of God.

There was a time when human beings heard or at least desired to hear the music of the planets. In fact, the teaching of astronomy in medieval universities began with a course on music because to the medieval mind the connection among all the harmonies of creation was vital and real.[6] That sense still needs to be nurtured today. Life is spiritually impoverished when a sense of the presence of the holy is no longer cultivated. Such cultivation is part of the spiritual formation of the pastor, which can be concretely expressed in a journal.

J. Barrie Shepherd is a pastor and poet who works intentionally at identifying and writing down divine self-disclosure in the ordinary events of daily life. He tells of moving into the study at a new parish assignment and wanting to see if the old fireplace in that study would still work. When he couldn't get the damper to open, he called on the church sexton and together they began to free up the damper with chisel and hammer. Finally working it free, they noticed that the first thing coming down the chimney was a moldy pigeon feather, followed by several others and then a wide assortment of debris that had been locked in the chimney for fifty years. The result of Shepherd's reflection on this experience is the poem that follows.

CHIMNEY CLEANING

What's the point
of a nice study with a fireplace, I ask you,
if the bricks have never darkened under woodsmoke,
nor reflected warm and dancing fingers
against your hands and face?
First the damper must be opened to the sky
and it's stuck tight. Just tap it here
and here to set it free. Now see, a scattering
of dust, then more and more; the dull dead weight
of fifty years begins to fall; the dry,
long-dead detritus of a vacant space
unknown to all but pigeons.

They appeared, at first,
in fragments—a skull, a wizened claw
and shattered wing—then, as the gap grew wider,
entire birds, or rather skeletons of birds, eggs
too,
perhaps a baker's dozen, smeared in withered yolk.
Discovering Dachau might have seemed somewhat
like this. The stumbling shock of corpses
heaped on corpses, dry, dessicated mayhem curled
and crumpled by decay, yet still surprising
structured delicate from bone to fragile bone,
and with shreds of skin, the odd, ironic feather
to recall the whirr of wings in flight
against the lifting wind.

What brought them to this
tumbling, bleak reverse of resurrection?
Had they flown here at the last to lay them down
and die beside the soothing winter warmth of oil
heat?
Might it have been those baffles added years ago
to shut out gusty winds that trapped a colony
to wait a long, pedestrian death, their wings
battering
the prison walls to rise and fall continually,
until
the broken feathers could no longer bear them
up out of the choking dust?

Whatever, there they lay, disclosed
like quail or manna fallen in the desert, food
for thought, at least, and poetry perhaps.
All things considered, it's not everyone who
writes
his sermons, says his prayers, crafts poems hard
beside a pigeon cemetery. Who, then, might sit
beyond these other walls? And what might he
be thinking, writing, praying?[7]

This poem demonstrates the power and grace that
can be experienced in the disciplined observation
and recording of events that seem to be touched in

elusive but potentially revelatory ways. After all, if John Wesley had not gone home and recorded in his journal his experience of going down to the Moravian meeting at Aldersgate where he felt his heart strangely warmed, we probably would know nothing of the experience. But because he wrote down his encounter with the holy and reflected upon it in a disciplined way, many people have been blessed and encouraged on their own faith pilgrimages. Further examples of how to observe and become aware are found in Wesley's published volumes, some of which contain his letters and journals.

Most experiences aren't as dramatic as Wesley's or as creative as Shepherd's, but neither do they need to be in order to justify the time and effort it takes to record them and reflect upon them. What is important to remember and to keep clearly in focus is the unique responsibility and opportunity of every human life. The gospel is spoken with a precise accent in each believer's life. That is why reflection upon experience is important to spiritual formation. The one thing no other person has is one's own experience of God.

Finally, it is important to write down enough to remember what it was that wasn't going to be forgotten. Journal entries like "Sunset on beach" or "woman with baby" most likely won't help too much when they are returned to later. It is important to write down enough detail so as to recall what was important in the event or experience. Such an entry doesn't need to be lengthy but it does need to evoke the important images and details of the event so that they can be recalled in the present moment.

Rather than writing simply "woman with baby," record the location, who was present, the emotions that were stirred at the time, and what, if any, scriptural reference or life situation seemed to be related to the experience. By following such a method, the essence of an experience can be captured using only a few words. Here is an entry from my own journal as an example:

"July, 1984. Cool summer evening. Freshly cut grass. Early stars coming out. Family picnic at our neighbors'. Pleasant conversation and rising laughter. The swelling in my heart at seeing a grandmother carrying an infant in her arms around the backyard at dusk, counting fireflies. Gratitude. Longing. Peace."

That journal entry made it into a sermon the next month, commemorating the fortieth anniversary of the bombing of Hiroshima, Japan, on June 6, 1945. It was one of a series of images in that sermon used to emphasize the point that to be grateful for life and to have a sense of wonder and amazement at being alive is a strong and central motivation toward world peace. I had no idea how or even if I would ever refer to that experience when I wrote it down. But I did know that it had touched me to see that new-born, vulnerable baby in her grandmother's arms, a grandmother and a baby doing what they have done together for generations. There was something holy and hopeful in that experience that I wanted to preserve and be able to recall as something for which I was grateful and which someday also might be a blessing to others.

Being a perceptive observer and recorder of experience honors the presence of Christ in daily life through a contemplated appreciation of creation and of God's continuing presence and activity in it and through it.

How to Write It Down

Keeping a journal is more than keeping daily diary entries as my grandmother did for nearly eighty years. In her diary she recorded such things as: "April 10, 1946—rained all day today—Edna came for lunch," and "August 11, 1966—Ben died. Funeral on Saturday," and "March 2, 1980—saw my first robin of the spring today. Last year it was March 15." Such diary entries are mostly information, although some of them, like "Ben died," could easily enough awake memory and emotion. The intent, however, is to chronicle events, not to record impressions about them. This is an appropriate function of a diary.

A journal adds a dimension lacking in a diary. Its intent is to record more than information. It also attempts to record response to experience. A diary entry might read, "Ruth came by the office at 10 this morning." A journal entry might read, "Ruth was waiting at the office when I got there again today. I felt irritated the minute I saw her. Why, I wonder? She's pleasant enough. But I honestly did feel put out by her being there. Thinking of my reaction to her reminded me of Henri Nouwen's comment about the priest who was similarly irritated until it dawned on him that his interruptions were his work." The diary entry records information only. The journal entry records information plus reflection upon the experience to which that information refers. The presence of Ruth was more than a statement of fact. It was a dynamic encounter that resulted in significant insight.

Not every experience needs to be recorded and reflected upon. But some experiences do have an edge on them or a spark to them which merits reflection. Remember, however, how fragile the memory of such experiences can be. Write them down. At least write down those that are the most impressive or the most troubling. They are the ones which offer the most potential for spiritual growth.

A more demanding and systematic use of journaling is that suggested by the method of Ira Progoff in his work *At a Journal Workshop.* The intent of such journaling is a much more exacting and disciplined plotting of the interior life than that which is being suggested here. However, having followed a modification of Progoff's method in leading a small bereavement group in the parish, I have found it to be a helpful and useful tool. This form of journaling may be of interest to pastors who would like to explore the interior life, including reflection upon dreams, more deeply. Those who are interested in more detailed information should read Progoff's work.[8]

The less systematic form of journaling being suggested here is perhaps more easily sustainable over a period of time. The keeping of such a journal requires only a bound volume of some kind, a pencil or pen, a quiet time and place, and the desire to record and reflect upon experience. Entries in such a journal do not need to be made daily. But to be helpful they should be made regularly. Such entries are intended neither for later publication nor for anyone else's reading. They are simply markers on one's own spiritual pathway. I've kept such a journal, more or less regularly, for fifteen years. Among other things it bears the record of my experiences with the deaths of loved ones, my dreams, changing parishes, conflict with and affirmation from members, joys and disappointments in family life, building a house, turning forty, and adopting a child.

Keeping such a journal can serve as a chronicle and as a tool in spiritual formation. In it one can be honest and clear with oneself in a way that may not yet be possible in actual relationships with others. Often I've experienced, in reflecting on an experience or a decision in my journal, greater clarity about the matter and distance from it, which helps me decide whether to discuss it with others or keep my own counsel. Either way, the keeping of a journal is a clarifying discipline. At times it can channel energies correctly. At other times it can correct misconceptions. And at all times it can lead to better self-understanding and to better understanding of others and of one's relationship to them and to God.

CHAPTER FOUR

Prayer as
Spiritual Formation

Prayer is a disciplined dedication to paying attention.
Without the singleminded attentiveness of prayer we will
rarely hear anything worth repeating or catch a vision worth
asking anyone else to gaze upon.
—JOHN WESTERHOFF

Gardner Taylor tells of how he once was walking around in the old chapel at Harvard where he came upon a plaque with a line from Ralph Waldo Emerson on it, "Acquaint thyself with deity." Taylor said that such instruction awed him. Nevertheless, "Acquaint thyself with deity" is appropriate counsel for the pastor. Without such acquaintance there is little to sustain and renew the life of one called to give aid, consolation, and guidance to the lives of others. Such an acquaintance with deity is at the heart of the pastor's spiritual life. There is an intentionality about it that calls for the disciplined spiritual exercise of intercessory prayer and the reading of scripture and devotional literature. How the pastor can approach the cultivation of such an acquaintance with deity is the theme of this chapter.

The Pastor and Prayer

A story is told concerning the noted preacher of London's City Temple, Leslie Weatherhead, that he once offended a wealthy matron by not offering a table grace before eating dinner in her home. She mentioned this offense to him, to which he reportedly replied, "Madam, my life is a prayer." He understood that prayer is related to the desire to live in the presence of Christ, thus experiencing each moment as a holy moment transformed by Christ's presence. To live with such awareness is to live a life of prayer. Such an understanding also influences and guides the thought, conversation, and action of the person who is aware of that influence in daily life. It brings one to the realization that even the most ordinary moments and experiences are bearers of the holy. The ability to see the presence of the holy in the ordinary is, in part, what it means to pray without ceasing.

For the pastor there is a necessary relationship between active ministry and prayer. Wilhelm Lohe, in describing this relationship, writes,

> Whoever must always give must always have; and since he cannot draw out of himself what he must give, he must ever keep near the living fountain in order to draw . . . The fullness and concentration of life is a praying heart. Solitude is the fountain of all living streams, and nothing glorious is born in public.[1]

Cotton Mather also was aware of this relationship between active ministry and prayer. He once quoted a preacher of his day whom he held in high regard as saying,

God will sense that man's labors that lumbers up and down the world all week and then upon Saturday in the afternoon goes into his study, whereas God knows that time were little enough to pray and weep in, and get his heart into a fit frame for the duties of the approaching Sabbath.[2]

Having stated something of the importance of the place of prayer in the pastor's devotional life, we turn now to specific aspects of that life of prayer: integrity, regularity, form, and content. These aspects help establish and maintain that place in the pastor's daily life.

Integrity

How much of the praying of pastors is primarily public prayer, that is, the pastoral prayer of the Sunday morning liturgy? Likely it is more than some would care to admit. Yet there are ramifications connected to such limited, utilitarian use of prayer. First among these is an internal sense of discontinuity in the pastor. The internal life and the external life are not in harmony. This is true, of course, of anyone's life. However, the pastor must deal with a sense of spiritual dishonesty about this discontinuity in a way that most other people don't have to. This is because most people who seldom pray in private seldom have to present themselves in public as though they do. There is, however, an expectation that the pastor has been praying in private.

Often the pastor represents the people in their need before God eloquently and graciously in the pastoral prayer offered on Sunday morning, and such public pastoral prayers are not without their proper and helpful effect. They can be channels of grace and healing, as at their best they ought to be. The concern here is not their effect on the people but their effect on the pastor. If the pastor lives with an awareness of this discontinuity between public expressions and private realities in his or her own prayer life, then that pastor stands in need of correction and redirection. No matter how eloquent or efficacious the public prayers of such a pastor may be, the inner life of that pastor remains in need of growth and healing.

A second ramification of the primarily utilitarian use of prayer is its lack of inner depth. Such inner depth is sensed in the life of the person who has struggled to pray faithfully in private. But often it is lacking in the life of the person who prays only in public. Importance lies in the person doing the praying, not just in the words that person uses in prayer. The way the images are formed and even the way the sounds of the words are made in public prayer is related to the life of personal devotional prayer. When one has prayed for someone in private, praying for that same person in public becomes a deeper experience. There is continuity between the words of the prayer and the life of the person who speaks those words. Such internal continuity and spiritual honesty in the life of the pastor can be sustaining even in moments when prayer, either public or private, is experienced as shallow or barren. In such moments the pastor can know that the goal has been to pray faithfully, however the actual experience may feel at the time. God knows the intent of the heart, even when the most honest prayer that can be offered is the desire to be a faithful servant in weary or barren times. Such a desire to be faithful is the linchpin of commitment in a personal devotional life. If how one happens to feel about prayer on a given day is at the center, then the

and limitations. There are times when rest is a more responsible and faithful choice than compulsively following scheduled devotional time.

Clearly, there needs to be flexibility within regularity in the devotional life. But such flexibility isn't license to pray only when one wants to or has the time. It is rather an acknowledgment of physical and mental limitations and of the sometimes demanding nature of pastoral work. However, the need for flexibility normally describes the exception rather than the norm. If it doesn't, an honest and serious look at how one is ordering one's time is indicated. To be always available to everyone is, in a sense, never to be truly present to anyone. A necessary part of ministry for others is time spent in solitude for oneself and for them.

Regularity is not bondage, it is commitment. It is a clearly defined time set aside specifically for a personal devotional life. It doesn't necessarily have to be every day, although that is the recommended practice here. The key is that it be a regular discipline given clear priority at specific times during the week. It needs to have the same sense of urgency and importance as do those blocks of time on the weekly calendar marked "hospital calls," "sermon preparation," and "Wednesday evening committee meetings." Without blocks of time marked "prayer," many busy pastors will simply fill those blocks with something else, such as "Drive Alice to the nursing home board meeting." Such aspects of ministry have their proper and necessary place, but so does prayer. Without intent and commitment to regularity in this aspect of ministry, it can become lost in the maze of other activities in the pastor's life.

There is a sense in which the priority of prayer

ought to be the first priority of the pastoral ministry. The pastor who says, "My people come first," needs to reflect theologically on that statement. A personal commitment to the tasks of pastoral care is not the same thing as a ministry centered in the love and presence of Christ. The former commitment can be self-serving and self-deceiving. The latter commitment is centered where it ought to be, in the sustaining presence and love of Christ.

Regularity in prayer is commitment to this central priority in ministry. Every pastor can learn to pray with clear intent, which can be encouraged by establishing goals for times of prayer. To go from a sporadic prayer life to an hour of prayer every day is probably not a realistic starting point. But to commit oneself, for instance, to forty-five minutes of pre-scheduled devotional time on Tuesday, Thursday, and Sunday is within reason and the grasp of even the busiest pastor. If it isn't, a review of priorities is in order.

For there to be times when the pastor isn't accessible to the people, times when the door to the study is closed because the pastor is praying, is not a faithless act. It is, rather, close to the heart of faithful pastoral care. In such moments of private intercession there can be a clarity of concern and compassion that isn't always so readily available in the proximity of physical presence and the press of human need.

Distance is an important ingredient in well-balanced, faithful pastoral care because distance allows space for pastor and parishioner alike. To be always and transparently present is at times to become too familiar. It is important for the people to know that the pastor has spent time alone in the presence of God, to know that the pastor has stood still on holy ground on their behalf.

Distance has a proper, necessary, and often neglected place in the pastoral office. But such distance also means there will be, at times, an element of loneliness and apartness in the pastor's life. This is in the nature of the work. Surely Moses, Jeremiah, and Paul knew such moments, as did Jesus himself. To choose to spend time in the presence of the holy is not the way of the world and will not soon be recognized, valued, or understood. But it is the way of faithfulness. And out of it flows the ability to be present to and for others in the ensuing moments of active ministry in the world.

Times of solitude and prayer do not detract from the tasks of active ministry; they deepen and enrich them. Having spent time alone with God in prayer clarifies and deepens the quality of time, the quality of care, and the quality of prayer that is offered from the altar, at the hospital bedside, or in the counseling session. To be regular in such times set aside for prayer is not to be selfish. It is faithfully to fulfill a central task of the pastor's calling, which is to be an intercessor before God for those given into the pastor's spiritual care.

Form

Having set aside time to pray, we must ask how that time can best be ordered and filled. A repeatable form is a valuable aid in sustaining a continuing life of prayer. To be able to reenter a familiar, established form maintains continuity and focuses energy and time more immediately on prayer than on how to go about praying.

Balance is a key concept in the establishment of a format for prayer. Not all the time should be spent in any one area, such as confession, intercession, or praise. A balance among a variety of themes can help keep the life of prayer fresh and properly focused on a wide range of pastoral concerns, personal concerns, and concerns for the whole church and the human family. One way to ensure such balance is through proportionate amounts of time given to various aspects of the devotional life. Take, for instance, the forty-five minute block of time mentioned earlier. How are those minutes best spent? There are times, of course, when all forty-five minutes will be spent in confession or in intercession or praise, depending on circumstance and need. However, a more typical balance in a continuing and sustainable devotional life might look something more like the following.

Begin the period with fifteen minutes of Bible reading, balanced between Old Testament and New Testament. One suggestion is to read one psalm each day coupled with one chapter from a book of the Bible. If this pattern is followed, the entire psalter can be read through twice each year and several biblical books can be read in their entirety. Such a method holds the added benefit of enabling large portions of scripture to be read over a sustained period of time, thereby nurturing a richer sense of the story of a given book as well as its relationship to the larger story of the Bible. In addition to deepening the personal devotional life of the pastor, reading in this manner can also broaden the base of the preaching and teaching ministry. The pastor spends more time with the Bible and develops an understanding, through regular reading, of its rich and diverse themes rooted in its foundational stories of creation, commission, redemption, and witness.

The second fifteen minutes could be devoted to the reading of devotional literature and the use of prayers found in anthologies of prayer and to reading selections from devotional classics. There are several advantages to incorporating such resources routinely into the devotional life. First, the language and imagery of the prayers and readings is capable of nurturing the spiritual life of the reader in a manner one's own more limited and personal resources likely could not sustain over time. Second, the use of such resources can expand areas of interest and concern to include themes that might normally not be considered were one dependent solely on interior resources to sustain one's spiritual life. Generally such anthologies of prayers and readings incorporate concerns for the whole created order and the peace and redemption of all things in a way that guards against the narrower focus of a purely private spiritual life. Third, the disciplined use of such objective aids can also guard against the intrusion of single-issue concerns in the devotional life. Surely it is appropriate to pray for peace in the world, for instance, and this should be done regularly. But to pray for peace without praying for justice and to pray for justice without praying for mercy and to pray for mercy without first offering a prayer of confession is to truncate the spiritual life and rob it of integrity necessary to its wholeness.

The third fifteen-minute period is for the offering of personal intercessions. There are several ways to order these prayers. Begin with the realization that not everything can be prayed for, specifically, every day. Thus a repeatable ordering of themes is helpful.

Here, for instance, is one possible way of ordering such prayers each week:

Sunday...................... preparation of self and congregation for worship
Monday..................... the week's work and issues that need addressing in it
Tuesday..................... all marriages and families
Wednesday................. one's own family and intimate friends
Thursday................... the congregation
Friday....................... worldwide concerns
Saturday................... confession

During this same fifteen-minute period, intercessions may be offered, by name, for a given number of parishioners. A helpful tool for such intercessions is the parish directory. A general guideline is to pray for all the members whose names begin with a given letter of the alphabet, one letter a day, in sequence. Following such a format allows each member to be named in prayer several times a year—ideally once a month, less often of course if the membership is large. In addition, a separate list, composed of the names of persons with more immediate concerns such as hospitalizations, a death in the family, or important life decisions, may be clipped to the current page of the directory and intercession offered for these persons daily. The names on this list will change as the needs of the people change. A final act of devotion in this fifteen-minute segment can be a personally worded, daily repeated offering of oneself and the day's life to God. One of my prayers is: "Almighty and gracious God, I offer to you the chalice which is the life you have given to me. Cleanse and purify me by the power of your Holy Spirit and fill me with precious, fresh new wine of your Kingdom for the living of this day's life. In Jesus' name I pray and do now rise to live this day. Amen."

Content

Among the most helpful and accessible books available for use in daily prayer is John Baillie's *A Diary of Private Prayer*. Its format is that of morning and evening prayer for each day of the month, plus special morning and evening prayers for use on Sundays. Opposite each prayer is a blank page where personal intercessions may be noted. The morning prayers express praise and gratitude and openness to the leading of the Spirit in the day's life. The evening prayers are reflective, meditative, and confessional. Taken together they form a solid, dependable frame on which the life of personal devotion can be built.

A more recent prayer book, modeled on and influenced by the Baillie book, is J. Barrie Shepherd's *Diary of Daily Prayer*, which follows Baillie's format in having morning and evening prayers for each day of the month, plus special prayers for Sunday and blank pages opposite each prayer. Baillie's prayers are steeped in classical language and imagery. Shepherd's are more poetic and modern.

Volumes like these can be helpful tools in supporting a personal devotional life. They are not intended to be the whole of that life. Rather they can be helpful aids in providing a consistent and readily available series of images for prayer. They can help sustain a daily prayer discipline in those inevitable dry and barren seasons when there is little personal interest or energy available to sustain such a commitment. Other sources of devotional material that could be used during this fifteen-minute segment include pastoral anthologies and devotional classics. One

63

practical advantage of such resources is that brief meaningful passages can be read from them at a single setting. A second advantage is the spiritual depth and richness of their themes and images. I will mention several of these as examples of such resources currently available.

Perhaps the most complete pastoral resource of prayers and readings available is John W. Doberstein's *Minister's Prayer Book*, which is organized around seven themes in the life of the pastor, one for each day of the week. These themes are: the Divine Institution and Commission of the Ministry, the Promise and Responsibility of the Ministry, the Minister's Life, the Minister as Confessor, the Minister as Pastor, the Minister as Intercessor, and the Minister as Preacher. For each day of the week there also are suggested prayers for morning, noon, and evening use, as well as planned intercessions, confession, suggested Bible passages related to the day's theme, and other Bible passages for meditation. The anthology section for each day is composed of excerpts from the thought and writing of a variety of persons ranging over the centuries of Christian thought. Using one of the morning or evening prayers, along with a reading or two from the anthology each day, can help sustain balance in the pastor's vision of life and work and can comfortably be included within this fifteen-minute time frame.

A second such pastoral resource is *A Guide to Prayer for Ministers and Other Servants*, which contains material for daily prayer and meditation as well as material for monthly private retreats. Its format is that of weekly themes, which follow those established by the ecumenical lectionary. Its suggested format for daily devotion includes the following elements: invocation, psalm, scripture readings,

readings for reflection, prayers, reflection, and a hymn. The anthology readings offer diversity from Doberstein's selections in two helpful ways. First, they include the thought of more recent spiritual writers than does Doberstein. Second, the language in them is more inclusive. The Doberstein book is more comprehensive in scope and in reference to classical devotional literature. *A Guide to Prayer for Ministers and Other Servants* is more current in focus and more accessible to beginners in the discipline of spiritual devotion. Either book, however, is an excellent resource for the cultivation of a personal devotional life and both are readily available.

What is needed in the reading of devotional classics is method and patience. To have read one such book in the course of a year's time is much better than to have some general idea about many of them but never actually to have read one. Take, for instance, two books commonly known by title but not so commonly read: *The Imitation of Christ* by Thomas a Kempis and *The Confessions of Saint Augustine.* In my editions, *The Confessions* has three hundred forty-seven pages and *The Imitation of Christ* two hundred thirty-six pages. To read them through, cover to cover, requires commitment, time, and method. But the reading can be accomplished easily once a system for going about it is in place. The format of many of the devotional classics such as these two, makes them well suited for the reading of brief sections at a single sitting. Take, for instance, the format of *The Imitation of Christ.* Most of its thematic subsections are a page or two in length, three or four pages at the most. This format allows for the reading of a single section each day in two or three minutes of devotional time. Even allowing for several off days each week, the whole of *The Imitation of Christ* can be read in this manner over the course of five or six months. A similar practice is allowed by the format of Augustine's *Confessions*, where there are two hundred seventy-eight thematic subsections, sometimes two or more of them on a single page. Reading *The Confessions* at the rate of only a page a day makes possible a complete reading of the text in one year.

What is true of classical devotional literature is true of much modern devotional literature as well. Take, for instance, the twentieth-century devotional and pastoral writing of Reinhold Niebuhr and Dag Hammarskjöld. Niebuhr's *Leaves from the Notebook of a Tamed Cynic* and Hammarskjöld's *Markings* are examples of devotional literature that can be read following the same format as that described above. *Leaves from the Notebook of a Tamed Cynic* is composed of excerpts from Niebuhr's personal journal kept while he was a parish pastor in Detroit from 1915 to 1928. In the entries, Niebuhr considers many of the joys and sorrows of parish ministry, probes the nature of authentic faith, and illuminates some of the moral and ethical dilemmas of the pastor in conflict with the dominant prejudices of the day. The passage of nearly sixty years since its first publication has not diminished the timeliness of its message. Again, as do *The Confessions* and *The Imitation of Christ*, this devotional classic lends itself to reading brief passages at a single sitting. The journal entries are headed by the year from which they are taken. Each entry is rarely longer than one or two pages, sometimes only a single paragraph. If a single entry is read a day, the entire journal can easily be read in six months.

Dag Hammarskjöld's *Markings* follows a similar format in that its material is organized according to the years the entries were made. These entries are often several to a page and rarely longer than a page each, again allowing for brief but meaningful passages to be read at a single sitting. These passages are filled with severe personal honesty and penetrating spiritual insight. Hammarskjöld's intellectual ability and perception, his knowledge of art, science, poetry, literature, and history, add size, proportion, and depth to his writing. Reading a page of *Markings* a day can result, once again, in the completion of the entire book in six months.

If the reader follows the format suggested above, two devotional volumes can be read in a year's time by devoting only a few minutes a day to the reading. Thinking of the cumulative effect of such a commitment to reading devotional literature puts the possible long-term result of such a commitment in a favorable light. Say, for instance, such reading was begun at the age of forty and continued only until retirement at the age of sixty-five. During the course of those twenty-five years a minimum of fifty such devotional books would be read. This is a much more profitable outcome than the well-intended desire to sit down and read such a book one day, perhaps during Lent, but never actually getting around to it. Such a long-range commitment is sustainable over the long haul of years of active public ministry with its numerous other demands and expectations. What it requires is planning and discipline. The benefits of depth of spiritual insight, imagery, integrity, and growth are well worth the few moments a day necessary to do such reading.

CHAPTER FIVE

Reading the Bible

Diligently apply yourself to the reading of the sacred Scriptures. . . . For we who read the things of God need much application, lest we should say or think anything too rashly about them.

—ORIGEN

Why Read the Bible?

Central to any pastoral reading program is the reading and study of the Bible. There are, of course, various ways to read the Bible. It can be read as part of a personal devotional life, as literature, as information, or in an attempt to get up a sermon for the next Sunday. Each of these emphases has its own motives and can accomplish a purpose for the reader. However, reading the Bible with an eye primarily on an upcoming sermon frequently resists the clear guidance and instruction the Bible is intended to offer for the whole of life, the pastor's own life as well as the lives of others.

There is nothing wrong with reading the Bible and developing clear themes from that reading for preaching. The Bible should be the source for the development of such themes. Yet, reading the Bible solely, or even primarily, for such purposes can keep the pastor at arm's length from the address of the Word of God to the pastor's own life. The Bible then becomes a book like any other book, that is, helpful resource material from which to develop sermon ideas. This utilitarian use of the scripture can result in a gospel-centered sermon, but often only at the expense of the spiritual integrity of the pastor, who knows that the Bible has been used rather than allowed to address the pastor's own life directly. This is why reading the Bible devotionally, or at least independently of the search for sermon texts, is a helpful spiritual discipline for the pastor. After all, that is how the people in the pews read the Bible, as guidance for their lives.

Sermons based on the Bible should be constructed from careful exegesis of appropriate biblical texts. But that is another matter. The emphasis here is on reading the Bible personally and devotionally, using a systematic approach that allows for reading broader portions of scripture than would normally be read when the purpose is primarily the seeking of a preachable text.

The central place of the Bible in Christian devotional life needs to be reclaimed both by liberals, who often have abandoned it in favor of books about the Bible, and by conservatives, who by narrow interpretations often limit its real authority, guiding grace, and wise council. Not to read the Bible at all or to read it too narrowly can rob it of the actual guidance and instruction it has to offer Christians attempting to live faithfully in the world today.

In writing of the importance of reading and studying the Bible, Luther once stated,

Let us not lose the Bible, but with diligence, in fear
and invocation of God, read and preach it. While that
remains and flourishes, all prospers with the state;
'tis head and empress of all arts and faculties. Let but
divinity fall, and I would not give a straw for the rest.[1]

The central place given to reading the Bible in the
pastor's life needs to be supported by method and by
discipline if it is to be sustained over the years and to
overcome the variety of temptations and distractions
that arise to discourage such a commitment. At one
time or another many pastors have made the same
commitment some of their parishioners, well-intended but neither well informed nor well guided,
have made: to read the Bible from cover to cover. The
resulting experience is also probably shared by
many: They start out strong in Genesis, remain
interested through Exodus, bog down in Leviticus,
and quit in Deuteronomy. What is lacking is not good
intention, or even discipline necessarily, but rather
method and guidance for the task.

Both discipline and method are important to any
informed and sustained reading of the Bible. Theologian Joseph Sittler describes an order to the spiritual
life that demands discipline. Although the discipline
is necessary it does not need to be the same thing at
the same time for everyone. Yet there must be such
discipline, given our human leaning toward the lack
of it, especially so perhaps in reading the scripture
and in prayer. Sittler comments, for instance, on the
discipline of pre–Vatican II Roman Catholic priests,
who could be seen on trains and buses with black
prayer books or missals, reading the Psalms every
day, and all of them in the course of the week, as they
were obliged to do. Sittler describes the importance
of such disciplined reading as a way of letting the
language of the Bible sink in and its images percolate.

Discipline and method are key elements in a sustained reading of the Bible over the long haul.[2]

Method and Discipline in Bible Reading

Our focus now turns to the development of a purposeful, disciplined approach to reading the Bible with some measure of balance and possibility of continuing on beyond the first few days of a well-intended desire.

A first observation is to note the importance of reading large enough portions of scripture to develop a sense for the movement of God's grace across the pages of a story. Taking smaller and smaller bites limits this sense of the greater story of salvation found in the Bible. When reading from Ruth for instance, it is important to know her whole story and not just the moving passage about her devotion to Naomi (Ruth 1:16-18). Reading this passage in the context of Ruth's whole story leads the reader away from a sentimental reflection on family loyalty to a sobering consideration of the outright abuse of women, their need and their poverty in a male-dominated Hebrew culture, that led to the vulnerability of widows like Orpah, Naomi, and Ruth. That's a different lesson altogether. It becomes possible only with a broader understanding of the whole story of Ruth. The same would be true of any biblical figure or theme. Even a familiar and loved verse such as "God is love" (I John 4:16) can best be understood from a perspective that is informed both as to its own exegetical context and to the whole movement of God's involvement in human affairs told in the stories of salvation history from Genesis through the Revelation to John.

Taking large enough bites of scripture is important,

but they do not need to be taken all at the same time. The idea of reading at regular intervals is more important than the amount of reading done at any one time. For example, it may take a month to read the twenty-eight chapters of Matthew, but reading them in sequence is the key to developing a broader sense for the whole of Matthew's story and particular point of view. In reading his Gospel in this way, for example, a commentary is not needed to inform the reader that *discipleship* is a key word for Matthew. That is discovered in reading and encountering Matthew's frequent use of the "follow me" theme in Jesus' ministry.

Pastors who follow the Consultation on Common Texts lectionary series for years A, B, and C would find it helpful to read the gospel appointed for the upcoming year in the month or so before its reading is publicly begun in the congregation on the first Sunday in Advent. This gives a renewed sense for the movement of the story in that gospel. It also serves as an aid in planning a sequence of preaching and teaching themes for the year.

In addition to the appointed lessons of the Consultation on Common Texts lectionary, there are several other readily available resources for guidance in developing a balanced and disciplined approach to reading the Bible. Several denominational service books and hymnals provide a sequential listing of pericope readings, as well as daily offices and a presentation of scriptural themes for the principal feasts, holy days, Saints' days, and Sundays of the church year. Typical daily office lectionary usage is modeled in the *Book of Common Prayer* of the Episcopal Church (pp. 934ff.) and in the *Lutheran Book of Worship* (pp. 179ff.). Devotional manuals also provide guidance in developing a disciplined approach to regular Bible reading. The *Minister's Prayer*

Book, edited by John W. Doberstein and recently revised (Philadelphia: Fortress Press, 1985), has been for several decades a valuable guide to a disciplined devotional life for pastors. It provides both the appointed lessons and additional lessons, revolving around seven principal themes in the minister's life and calling, for each day of the week. Another such manual is *A Guide to Prayer for Ministers and Other Servants* (Nashville: The Upper Room, 1983), which presents daily scripture readings related to and supportive of a specific theme in ministry for each week of the church year. Another and perhaps the most readily available and economical guide for scripture reading is to be found in the quarterly daily devotional guides located in the tract rack of many congregations. Following such a guide offers the advantage of keeping the pastor in touch with the scriptural themes, images, and interpretations that are nurturing the spiritual lives of many lay people.

An additional aid to the development of disciplined Bible reading is to relate at least some of the reading to a pastor's pericope study group that meets on a regular basis to discuss prearranged texts for the next Sunday. Some pastors can be assigned texts for exegetical development in the group, while other pastors may be asked to share experiences or images from reading and life that can enrich and enliven the preaching and teaching possibilities of these texts for all the members of the group. Such a collegial setting offers a disciplined method of accountability and mutual support that can bear healthy fruit in the life of pastor and congregation alike.

How to Read the Bible Devotionally

The purpose of reading the Bible devotionally is to open oneself to the transforming presence of God. At this level of the spiritual reading of scripture the significant word is encounter, not information. Through such reading an encounter with God takes place and life is given a new vision that accords with God's purposes. It begins to be shaped by openness to God and obedience to God's will. The whole purpose behind such encounter with God in spiritual reading of the scripture is that those who read the Word may become, in their actions and relationships, what God intends them to be.

The traditional approach to evangelical meditation on the scripture is known by its classical name *lectio divina* or spiritual reading. In the tradition of Luther, this *lectio divina* included the practices of *meditatio, tentatio,* and *oratio,* that is, *meditation, self-examination,* and *prayer.* Other traditions add the practices of *lectio* (reading the text) and *contemplatio* (contemplation of the text) to *lectio divina.* Such practices have guided Christian spiritual reading of the Bible for centuries. Robert Mulholland has insightfully bracketed these traditional practices with *silencio* (silence) at the beginning and *incarnatio* (the word active in life) at the end.[3]

It is appropriate to begin the spiritual reading of scripture in silence so as to allow time for an inner opening of the heart and mind toward God. Such focusing does not come easy. There are often distractions. The real discipline of *silencio* takes place as the heart and mind become uncluttered and the body relaxed so as to be as present as possible in that moment of self-recollection. Then it becomes possible to read the text *(lectio)* with an open heart and listening ear and not simply to bring one's own agenda of questions and concerns to it. The basic concern in *lectio* is not with how much scripture is read but with how attentive the reader is to that which is read. *Meditatio* is where the reader begins to struggle with the meaning of the passage as it addresses his or her own life. This can be painful because it is here the reader discovers that his or her life often is not in harmony with what God intends it to be. If *meditatio* is hearing what God is saying to the reader, then *oratio* is the reader's response to God. It may be a painful, joyful, penitent, or grateful response, depending upon the experience of the reader in *meditatio*. In any event it is characterized by honest response to the Word that has been received. Next the reader simply waits upon the Lord in quietness *(contemplatio)*. The discipline here is to become available and responsive to the will of God and to yield to it concretely in daily life *(incarnatio)*.

The practice of *lectio divina* is intended to deepen the reader's response of faith in God and faithful discipleship in life. It is much more than the seeking of correct information from the scripture. It is the spiritual discipline of placing oneself under the authority of the God who is revealed in the scripture and then living responsively under the rule of that God in the world.

Techniques for Reading the Bible Effectively

Numerous approaches to reading the Bible have evolved over the centuries. Three of those techniques will be discussed here as suggestive of the rich variety of approaches available to the reader of the scripture.

First, consider reading at least selected portions of the Bible aloud. After all, much of the biblical material was first received by the earliest Christian communities orally. One copy of a letter from Paul would arrive at Corinth or Ephesus and then would be read aloud to the gathered community. This is the conception of some biblical scholars, such as Charles Tolbert of Vanderbilt, who say that the form and structure of some New Testament books appears to assume a listening rather than a reading audience. And there is an additional dynamic at work when the written word is spoken aloud. The response of the ear is added to the response of the eye, and the word becomes more alive for both listener and speaker. This can be true not only in the context of public reading of scripture at worship but also in the pastor's devotional and professional reading as well. It is especially helpful, having selected a text for Sunday, to read it aloud several times. This helps give clarity to its actual content and to the places of emphasis that seem to fall naturally as the passage is read aloud. Whatever natural rhythm or movement may be present can be much more readily sensed when reading aloud.

An obvious additional benefit to following this discipline is the improvement of the reading of the text aloud during Sunday morning worship. The words, the pauses, the rhythm, the cadence of the language as it is expressed through the reader's voice and spirit in the moment of addressing God's word to the lives of the listeners all become channels of grace for them. Then is when speaking becomes more than conveying information. It becomes a holy moment of address and not simply because the reader can read well or has a pleasant voice. Rather it becomes a word of holy address because the reader has personally listened to that word and stands under its authority as one whose charge it is to deliver it faithfully to others. Reading the Bible aloud, in public or in private, can enhance public worship and deepen the spiritual life of speaker and hearer alike.

When the pastor has listened to the word in the study, it will have life and vitality at the lectern and in the pulpit that perhaps cannot be described but will be known.

Second, it is helpful to read the Bible with what Paul Ricoeur calls a certain "naivete," that is, with a certain degree of playfulness of mind and spirit before the hard work of exegesis begins, which often can rob the Bible of its personal address to the reader. It is helpful to approach the reading of the Bible with an openness to the images, memories, and questions the reading evokes. That is frequently the primary way the people to whom the lesson will be read experience it, how it affects them personally. To read the Bible in this way can be personally stimulating for spiritual growth and practically helpful for the development of creative, textually rooted images for preaching, teaching, and counseling ministries.

A third technique for Bible reading is that developed by Ignatius Loyola. It uses an imaginative approach to the scripture. The basic principle is to imagine oneself as present in the scene the text is describing and to ask certain questions of the text and of oneself from that point of view. Who is identified most closely within the text? What is seen most clearly? What are the sounds? The smells? What is the unspoken action behind and within the stated action? Can the unspoken responses of the participants be imagined? What might one's own responses have been?

These kinds of questions addressed imaginatively to the text help engage the heart as well as the mind of the reader to the present dynamic reality of the text for the reader's own life. Such questioning of texts can help enliven them for the reader and help sustain interest in continuing, disciplined reading of the

Bible. Most people, pastors included, are more interested in something they themselves are part of. Identifying oneself somewhere in the text gives one a stake in it. It is no longer simply information about what happened to somebody else one time. The reader is there, or realizes she easily could have been had she been alive then. Another benefit, besides the interest generated by personal identity, is the increased hesitancy to rail against the "bad guys" in the text indiscriminately; for example, "Why didn't those Pharisees accept Jesus' counsel?" In all likelihood the reader could have been one of them and, in the interest of self-preservation, forced to consider at the very least an argument supporting Pharisaic resistance. Such identification of self in the text may help keep the reader from the temptation to ask condescendingly, "What's the matter with those Jews in this text? Can't they see who Jesus is?" Well, probably not and understandably so, as the reader would have discovered had he been one of them listening to Jesus draw into question some of the Jews' most deeply held beliefs and the religious values sacred to their forebears.

Reading the Bible aloud, with a certain initial naivete and imaginatively, can enliven and enrich one's own spiritual life, add depth and compassion to the pastoral ministry, and expand the possibilities for preaching images before one ever turns to a volume of illustrations and sermon aids to glean someone else's learnings from the text. Often those who spend time with the Bible discover that their own images and those of the text itself provide the most lively and appropriate illustrations for their ministries of preaching, teaching, and pastoral care.

CHAPTER SIX

Reading as
Spiritual Formation

*What has exceedingly hurt you in time past, nay, and I fear, to
this day, is, want of reading.*

—JOHN WESLEY

Identification

Reading can expand the capacities of the heart and
the mind and nurture understanding, compassion,
and identity with other people. It was Willa Cather in
O Pioneers! who said there are only two or three
human stories and they go on repeating themselves
as fiercely as if they had never happened before. That
is one reason why there is great power in literature. It
is the power of identification with the themes of
common human experience developed in the lives of
the characters. Such identification, through reading,
adds the quality of necessary distance to pastoral
reflection about life that normally is not available
when reflecting only upon one's own experience.

Reflection on personal experience is appropriate
and necessary to professional and spiritual growth,
and it is best done in a continuing and disciplined

manner, as discussed in the sections on journaling in chapter 3. Reading broadens and enriches this purposeful discipline of reflection. Good literature gives voice and image to important dynamics of common human experience that otherwise might remain locked up inside, felt and somehow vaguely known, but incapable of being expressed in any way concretely helpful either to oneself or to others.

Reading good literature helps relate universal human experiences to one's own experience. When an author powerfully, with precision in description of time and circumstance, describes the longing or the greed or the fear in a single human being's heart, that author is describing something in anyone who has ever known longing or greed or fear. There is power in such identification that can be used effectively in one's own life and in helping others better understand their lives as well.

The great single power in literature is the power of identification. It is this dynamic that grips those who read books. They are in this thing too. Such reading can deepen, enable, and grace life with increased capacity for human sympathy, self-understanding, and identification with others. Anyone who has ever had the experience of reading late into the evening or has resisted coming to the end of a compelling story has had an experience of such personal identification, which can enrich one's own perception of and contribution to the lives of others.

Resistances to Reading

Yet at times a pastor can be heard saying, "I just don't have time to read," or "When I take time to read something I feel guilty and think I should be out there working." These are among the reasons likely to be mentioned by pastors when they are explaining why they don't read much. Some admit that the only regular reading they do is whatever is necessary to prepare a sermon for the coming week. This is a great loss both for the pastor and for the people that pastor serves.

Spending time with people is an important part of a pastor's work but it isn't the only important part of it. Reading is also important. Words and ideas are the tools of the pastor's trade. They are what pastors use to communicate the gospel to others. Reading is not optional for the pastor who desires to be competent and faithful. It is essential. In a letter to a pastor dated August 7, 1760, John Wesley clearly stated the importance of reading:

> What has exceedingly hurt you in time past, nay, and I fear, to this day, is, want of reading. . . . Whether you like it or no, read and pray daily. It is for your life; there is no other way; else you will be a trifler all your days. . . . Do justice to your own soul; give it time and means to grow. Do not starve yourself any longer.[1]

If reading is so important in the pastor's life, why is it sometimes resisted? One reason is that reading can be hard work, which often does not have an immediate payoff in terms of Sunday's sermon or a solution to a pastoral counseling or administrative problem. The motivation for disciplined reading needs to be deeply rooted if it is to be maintained. It rarely results in accolades from lay people. Yet it is important for the pastor to realize that being alone in the study is a significant form of ministry for the people being served. Out of such reflective solitude, as well as out of community, faith is forged and strengthened.

A second reason reading is resisted is that it can lead to giving up a long-held prejudice or cherished piece of misinformation. It is like the pastor who recounts being on a tour in the Holy Land, standing with a group outside the door of a church waiting their turn to enter. The group in front of them was a large group of church folk from congregations in Oklahoma and Texas. Their guide was another pastor, who was telling them, quite confidently, that on the very spot where they were standing Jesus had stood and in that very room Jesus had spoken. When it was the second group's turn to enter the church, their guide, a graduate student from a local university, began to explain the various architectural influences from different historical periods evident in the room. He went on to say that this current building had replaced another building, which had replaced another building, and that perhaps Jesus had once walked and spoken in that place. When the guide finished a woman whispered, "I wish I'd been in the other group."[2] Her wish is understandable. No one likes to have personal prejudices upset by the facts. But the pastor must be willing to do so. To gain a new understanding often means giving up a dearly held old one. That can be painful and costly but it can also be part of the process of growth. Reading can lead to such growth.

A third reason reading is resisted is the belief that experience is the real teacher in life. This is only partly true. Experience is a valuable teacher and much can be learned from it. Yet, no experience is really ever complete until it is reflected on. The task of interpretation, which is central to the work of the pastor, requires such reflection upon experience. The tools for that reflection include reading and study, which are, themselves, forms of experience, not substitutes for experiences with people in other dimensions of pastoral work.

Pastors who rely only on their personal experiences for growth and insight soon begin to lack the distance and perspective necessary for personal growth and for healthy relationships with other people. The perspective nurtured by reading and study offers a necessary balance to that of the practical experiences of pastoral ministry. Such a balance between reflection and engagement is healthy and helpful to pastor and lay people alike.

Why Read at All?

People read for a variety of reasons. Some read to get ahead. Some read for pleasure. Some read because they have to. Such reasons have their proper place. For the pastor, an appropriate response to the question, Why read? is, To expand the heart and the mind, to have a heart with more room in it and a mind with greater capacity.

Reading increases knowledge and deepens identification with and sympathy for the human condition and the created order. This is especially true of literature in which universal themes of our human experience are powerfully presented. Take, for example, the theme of Dostoevski's *Crime and Punishment,* a novel that addresses the harsh grip of guilt and the transforming possibility of redemption. Another example is Flaubert's *Madame Bovary,* where Emma, finally consumed by her lust and greed, is dying a painful death. A single thought there sums up the longing, pain, and selfishness in many a person's life: "A demand for money, . . . of all the winds that blow upon love, [is] the coldest and most destructive."[3]

Such literature isn't to be combed for teaching and preaching illustrations. It is to be read for the rich cadences in the language, the beauty of the images, the truths of human tragedy and joy it presents. Yet, reading a novel like *Madame Bovary* or *Crime and Punishment* also enriches the possibility of meaningful pastoral encounter in counseling and deepens pastoral sensitivity in preaching and teaching.

The popular American humorist, writer, and storyteller Garrison Keillor has developed two central dynamics of communication skill in his writing and speaking: (1) the importance of observation, and (2) the existence of the universal in the particular. He states these principles clearly near the end of *Lake Wobegon Days* when he observes, "Anything that ever happened to me is happening to other people. . . . Somewhere in the world right now, a kid is looking at something and thinking, 'I'm going to remember this for the rest of my life.'"[4] This insight is, in part, the genius of common human identity and, in part, an explanation of the power and popularity of storytellers and writers like Keillor. It also illustrates the evocative power of the familiar and the capacity to see the universality of the everyday experience of those who gather in the sanctuary on Sunday morning. One way to nurture such an awareness is through reading that touches the heart, the mind, and the memory. Such reading can broaden horizons and deepen sensitivities to those common threads of human experience that connect us all yet need to be given voice because although deeply felt often they cannot be clearly spoken. It is part of the pastor's work to give voice to such experience, feeling, and memory for others. And good literature is a well from which such words and images can be drawn to speak for those who often cannot speak for themselves.

How to Read Meaningfully

There are four steps in the process of meaningful study and reflection on life, whether through reading or observation. These four steps are repetition, concentration, comprehension, and reflection. Through repetition the mind can be channeled in a specific direction, which helps to ingrain healthy habits of thought. This does not mean repeating everything that has already been read but integrating key ideas from that reading into thought patterns. This is the same dynamic central to psychocybernetics which teaches the individual to repeat certain key affirmations regularly.

Concentration helps to focus attention and center the mind with a clear singleness of purpose. It can be enhanced by having a regular, uninterrupted time and place set aside for reading and study. This allows for easy return access to study with a minimum of set-up time. Such regularity serves as a reminder of the purpose of this particular time and place and of its importance.

Comprehension provides the base for an accurate perception of reality and leads to insight and discernment. It raises understanding to a new level. Underlining key passages or making marginal notes can be helpful techniques for improving comprehension.

Reflection defines the significance of what is being learned through reading and observation. It allows one to understand both the study material and oneself in relationship to it. A helpful form of reflection is the keeping of a journal of key learnings, with references to their source for return use or study at a later time.[5]

Pastors may consider forming a small study group, such as the kind suggested for pericope study in chapter 5. In such a group members can agree to read the same book over a stated period of time and meet to discuss it. Each member can assume responsibility for devising discussion questions for a given section of the book.

What to Read?

Making wise choices about what to read is an act of responsible stewardship. A helpful guideline for such decision making is to maintain a balanced reading program. Such a balance helps keep the pastor from becoming too narrowly focused in counseling, teaching, and preaching images. Images guiding a pastor's thinking and speaking ought to have enough diversity to enable the pastor to respond appropriately to a wide variety of human needs. If the images guiding a pastor come primarily from a single source, for example, newspapers, or biblical commentaries, or literature, the result can be an imbalance in thinking and narrowness of vision that limits the effectiveness of pastoral care. A helpful general guideline is to maintain a balance between the reading of fiction and non-fiction materials. Such balance can be maintained by reading two books concurrently, one a novel, for instance, and the other on some professional area of interest. Such reading can be accomplished without undue disruption because the themes and images of each book are distinct from one another. Also, most current professional books on ministry have clearly defined chapter and section headings, which allow for easy access to return reading. Such a pattern allows a balance to be maintained in thought processes and images that continue to nurture both the interior life and intellectual growth of the pastor.

At the end of this book is a suggested reading list for establishing a program of balanced reading. It is composed of several categories of both fiction and non-fiction. The categories provide the balance and the selections themselves are helpful as well for enriching and deepening the pastor's life.

CHAPTER SEVEN

Corporate Devotional Life

Nothing is so deadening to the divine as an habitual dealing with the outsides of holy things.
—GEORGE MacDONALD

One area that can bear healthy fruit for the pastor who nurtures a personal devotional life is public leadership of the life of the congregation. The focus of this chapter is on the pastor's spiritual leadership in the organizational life and corporate worship of the church.

Prayer in the Organizational Life of the Church

The temptation concerning prayer at meetings of church organizations and committees is to treat such prayer perfunctorily, as an icon of religious culture appropriate but not essential to the work to be done. "Pastor, would you lead us in prayer" is sometimes seen as another way of saying, "Well, I guess it's time to get started." Yet there is nothing essentially wrong with such a request. It is right and appropriate to seek God's guidance for the work of the church. The concern here is with the attitude and expectation with which such prayer is approached, especially by the one who has been asked to offer it. This is not a light-hearted matter and ought not to be approached glibly by the one who is to pray.

Corporate prayer is a priestly task of the pastoral ministry and needs to be approached with thoughtfulness, preparation, and pastoral sensitivity. Thoughtfulness means an attitude of awareness about the particular concerns of this group of people. Preparation means some prior thought about the purposes of this group and the tasks of ministry they have been charged to undertake. Pastoral clarity about these tasks, in a prayer for guidance and faithfulness, can help bring clarity to the people who are about to undertake them. Pastoral sensitivity means a moment's thought about the lives of the people who will overhear the prayer that is to be offered on their behalf. This doesn't mean that indiscreet revelations are offered in the prayer, such as, " . . . and help Evelyn at this time of difficulty in her marriage." Rather it means that the pastor acknowledges awareness of the continuing need for grace, strength, guidance, and sense of purpose that is always present in people, even when not consciously attended by them. That need can be attended by the pastor, whose task as a priest is to approach God, particularly for others.

Such thoughtfulness, preparation, and pastoral sensitivity need not be time-consuming. It is much more a matter of attentiveness and awareness. Yet it can have a significant effect in the life of the congregation in at least two ways. The first effect is the model of the pastor as a person of prayer. Demonstration is often the most helpful teacher. This is certainly the case, for instance, when I am attempting to wire a new light fixture. Reading the instructions about the various white, black, and ground wires is less effective for me than asking my father-in-law, a man more experienced in such tasks than I am, to show me what to do. Do not discount the practical worth of the observation of prayer.

People can benefit significantly from actually seeing and hearing what to do when it comes to the matter of prayer. They will, as they should, make their own adaptations and applications. However, the observation of a cattleman on the American frontier rings true with practical wisdom in this regard. Anticipating the long trail-drive from Texas to Montana with excitement and dread, he said simply, "Well, I reckon it's time to go . . . we'll never get there if we don't start."[1] Helping people start a life of prayer is one important thing the model of the pastor's own prayer life can do.

A second effect of the public prayer life of the pastor on the life of the congregation is less directly applicable but equally important. It is the encouragement of a disposition toward love and mutual concern in the community of faith. This can be just as well if not better accomplished by how the pastor approaches prayer as by the actual content of the prayers that are offered. It is important to hear the invitation to lead a group in prayer as a real seeking for spiritual guidance for the work at hand and to respond to that seeking with clear, focused, and honest intent. This response can be accomplished by following a few simple guidelines.

First, don't rush into the prayer. Allow for a time of settling and focusing before beginning to pray. This allows all present a moment to recollect themselves. It also allows the pastor time to consider what has been requested and to respond to that request appropriately, with grace and dignity and properly formed petition. The manner in which the pastor prepares for prayer and encourages others to prepare for prayer encourages depth and integrity in this frequent experience of life together in Christian community.

Second, when praying in such settings, consciously remember to whom the prayer is addressed. There is no place for glibly worded prayers offered with the primary intent of either getting them over with as soon as possible or with little apparent valuing of their importance. The pastor is the people's priest, the one who intercedes for them before God. This dimension of the pastoral ministry ought never to be taken light-heartedly, especially when a clear, public request for such prayer has been made. This doesn't mean that the request is always sincere. Sometimes church members in groups simply think they ought to pray, especially if the pastor is there. But that doesn't mean that the request needs to be responded to in kind. The pastor can instill a higher plain of spiritual vitality with a sincere response. When some common purpose, some sense of the presence of the holy, some evocation of the remembrance of past blessings, has been named and offered, both pastor and people alike know the prayer has not been perfunctory but a contemplated search for the mind of Christ.

Third, such public prayer in the organizations of the congregation ought also to have some specificity to it. This doesn't mean praying for guidance about the choice of paint colors for the church office. But it does mean being specific about guidance for the proper stewardship of that particular area of the church's ministry; for instance, " . . . and give us wisdom prudently, wisely, and fairly to manage the financial resources of this congregation. May we be mindful of the presence of Christ in our work and obedient to his will in our decision making. Amen."

These three guidelines for response to prayer requests in the organizational life of the church—settling and focusing time, awareness of the importance of the request, and some degree of specificity in the petition offered—can help the pastor model important aspects of a healthy spiritual life to members of the congregation in the recurring settings of its organizational life. People become what they know. Nurturing in them a knowledge of prayer as an important dimension of their developing wholeness in Christ is an important part of the pastor's role as the spiritual leader of a particular community of believers.

Praying in Corporate Worship Settings

Much of what has been said about leading prayers in the organizational life of the church also applies to leading the prayers of the people gathered for worship. However, the circumstances and to some degree the purpose of such liturgical prayer, are different. The same need for focusing, pastoral sensitivity, and specificity remains. But the dynamics of corporate worship are more complex, and thus the need for more inclusive images in prayer becomes more important. Because the setting is more diverse, the images evoking response and participation also must be more diverse so as to do their work within a wider overhearing by the people. In the corporate worship of a gathered congregation on Sunday morning, the unspoken but felt hopes and fears and longings of the whole people are present. The pastoral prayer needs in some way to acknowledge and give voice to this gathered, felt, but unarticulated longing.

Praying publicly and pastorally in such a setting isn't simple, nor is it easy. But it is an essential ingredient in the formation of healthy, mature, and responsible pastoral care. In this section we will deal with the dynamics of such pastoral prayer under three headings: (1) Content (the *What*); (2) Perception (the *Who*); and (3) Form (the *How*).

Content *(the* What)

First, note that the pastoral prayer is not a functional extension of the sermon. That is, it is not the place to say to the people what the pastor has not had the courage or clarity to say to them in the sermon. Such an approach lacks integrity and erodes the openness and trust that must be guarded and nurtured between pastor and people. The pastoral prayer, after all, is not addressed to them. It is addressed to God on their behalf and within their overhearing. And that is quite a different thing. To use the pastoral prayer to make theological pronouncements really addressed to the people instead of as an avenue of thanksgiving and intercession to God is dishonest and will often be sensed as manipulative. Even if not consciously intended as such, it can be just that, and when it is it erodes the function of thanksgiving and intercession in pastoral prayer. The direction of movement in the pastoral prayer must be clear. It is toward God from the pastor on behalf of the people.

What is true of sermons is also true of pastoral prayers; one cannot say everything each time one speaks, nor should one try to. There will be other Sundays, other sermons, other prayers. In the pastoral prayer it is better to focus, in a deliberately restrained way, on a single image or theme and some of its corollaries than to try to include every human need one can think of each time one prays.

If, for instance, the dominant message in the liturgy for the day has been focused on world hunger, then the pastoral prayer would be best developed around clusters of images having to do with various moral, economic, political, social, and theological concerns of a faithful Christian response to world hunger. Specific petitions for divorced persons, by comparison, might be offered more appropriately and helpfully on a Sunday when the liturgy has been focused on marriage and family concerns. It isn't that the pastor is unconcerned about divorced persons or the unemployed or the endangered environment. It is rather an acknowledgment of limitations and of the necessity of preparing the people and oneself for offering and participating in intercessions that are appropriate reflections and timely responses to the themes and issues addressed by the word and the liturgy on a particular Sunday.

The effective pastoral prayer should be constructed so that the themes of the scripture are clearly linked to the content of the sermon. Disciplined planning and restraint by the pastor will result in a clear and specific connection between scripture and the life setting of the people. At this point in the flow of worship, the people have heard the word read and preached and are now willing to respond to that word through prayer. The pastor's private devotional discipline of prayer and reading will help him or her focus on the primary connections between sermon, text, and life setting in the corporate prayers of the church.

Perception (the Who)

Having developed an understanding of the need for a clearly focused theme for the pastoral prayer, we focus now on considering those in whose presence that prayer will be offered. Obviously the prayer is offered in the presence of God, but it is also offered within the overhearing of the people gathered in the sanctuary. Awareness of their presence and attentiveness is another important dynamic in building a fuller understanding of and appreciation for the importance of the pastoral prayer.

For some people the pastoral prayer is the only one they will participate in all week. Others are struggling with how to pray, and they look to the pastoral prayer, perhaps unconsciously, for a model of prayer. Yet others have a need for someone to pray for them, but they are too hesitant or embarrassed to ask for such prayer. Some probably wish that pastoral prayer were not necessary because it adds two or three minutes to the worship service each week. All of these people are in the sanctuary on Sunday morning. The first step in the development of a sensitive pastoral prayer is the conscious awareness that they are there. The pastoral prayer is not a private prayer. It is a priestly act of intercession for all the gathered people, as well as for many who are not present, most of whom are not even known.

The pastor cannot possibly address the needs of each individual, for several common-sense reasons. First, they are not all known. Second, many of them involve pastoral discretion and have no place in public prayer. Third, there isn't time to include all the concerns within the limitations and goals of a

Sunday liturgy. Fourth, many of the individual needs are so narrowly focused as to be inappropriate in the circumstances of public corporate prayer. Yet all of these people are present, with their rich variety of needs and expectations for a pastoral response to those needs, in the gathered community on Sunday morning. Given the limitations and restraints already mentioned, how is the pastor to respond to them?

At the heart of the pastoral response in such prayer is a vision of the spiritual needs and longings most likely to be experienced, perhaps even commonly held in varying degrees, by the worshipers. For instance, every person present with a normal intellect has some degree of anticipation about the future and some recollection of past experience. Many have a sense of incompleteness and a need for the assurance of forgiveness and acceptance. Others surely are in need of healing, peace, or direction in their lives. Such themes as these, that is, hope, memory, fulfillment, forgiveness, healing, peace, and guidance, are universal enough and real enough for people to overhear and apply to their own personal situations. In other words, the people themselves bring the necessary interpretation to the prayer being offered on their behalf by the pastor. In this way they become intimate participants in the prayer without experiencing the violation of their private and painful concerns being publicly aired before the congregation. Instead, the pastoral prayer evokes their own personal responses, which they can then offer, in the privacy of their own hearts, within the course of the corporate prayer. In this sense, the function of the pastoral prayer is both intercession and evocation. The most powerful and helpful pastoral prayers are a healthy, intentional blend of these two dynamics, serving to nurture, encourage, and aid the spiritual life of the individual and the congregation.

Form (the How)

How is such a pastoral prayer, sensitive to the needs of the people and yet not so revelatory of specific needs as to be a violation of trust, to be formed for appropriate use in the circumstances of corporate worship? In this section we will discuss some of the limitations and advantages of so-called free and prepared pastoral prayers.

I use the description so-called free pastoral prayer deliberately because such prayer isn't always as free as perhaps the pastor envisions it to be. It is limited by the pastor's mental ability, spiritual insight and maturity, oral skill, and ability to think and speak clearly within the dynamic situation of a gathered community. It is also not altogether free of the potential for spiritual vanity and self-service on the part of the pastor. The temptation toward speaking eloquently at the expense of speaking faithfully is an ever-present hazard both in preaching and in praying.

One clear advantage of prepared pastoral prayers is that they provide the pastor time for honest self-assessment of motives informing the content of the prayer. This is a helpful spiritual exercise for the pastor to engage in on a regular basis. It disciplines thought, allows for proper spiritual reflection, and brings clarity to the actual content of the prayer to be offered. The poet John Donne expressed the importance of such spiritual preparation prior to the leading of public worship:

Since I am coming to that holy room
  Where with the choir of saints for evermore,
I shall be made Thy music; as I come
  I tune the instrument here at the door,
  And what I must do then, think here before.[2]

The discipline of prior thought and preparation for leading public prayer is as much an act of pastoral care and devotion as is the more spontaneous act of free pastoral prayer. It simply isn't true that carefully prepared prayers cannot be prayers of the heart. Rather, they are prepared in one setting, solitude, for delivery in another, corporate worship. That does not rob them of sincerity, depth, or sensitivity to human need. Time spent alone in the presence of Christ helps form the spiritual life of the pastor and influences the connection between the pastor who prays and the people on whose behalf the prayer is offered on Sunday morning. The people can often sense this connection, and it becomes a channel of grace for them. This is true, in part, because such careful attention results in a pastoral prayer of depth, clarity, and continuity that is regularly present in the spontaneous prayers of only a gifted few. The rest of us would do well, for ourselves and the people we serve, to tune our instruments at the door and to think clearly of what we must do before the time for actually doing it is upon us.

A second consideration for use of the pastoral prayer is to have it printed and placed in the bulletin. This option shares one disadvantage with the placement of printed scripture lessons in the bulletin. It limits the dynamic of interaction between orality and aurality when the word is spoken or prayer is offered. This is an important concern not to be dismissed too lightly. However, two advantages of having the printed prayer available help counterbalance this limitation. First, printed prayers allow for the possibility of participation by the people. Second, printed prayers become available as models of prayer and as spiritual resources in the lives and homes of lay people throughout the coming week. I remember a dying member of the congregation once telling me how important it was to her to have the prayer used in the sanctuary on Sunday available to her throughout the following week. It gave her a sense of connection to her friends and her church and a sense of contribution to the continuing ministry of the church to be able herself to offer that prayer again on each day of the new week. And a person doesn't have to be dying to sense the need for such connection and to feel the need for such a contribution to and for the church and the world. There are probably many people, who, if they weren't so embarrassed or inhibited, would say to their pastor, "Please teach me how to pray." The form and the content of a well-conceived pastoral prayer is a readily available current resource. With a little guidance and encouragement many people might use it regularly as part of their own devotional life.

To offer a prayer freely from the altar or pulpit has its place and there are times when such prayers are appropriate, powerful, and necessary. News of the sudden death of a congregational member would be such a time. But such occasions are more the exception than the rule. Besides, the faithful preparation of pastoral prayers on a regular basis provides excellent discipline and resources to draw upon when such occasions demanding spontaneity do arise. The depth of spontaneous prayer that comes forth from a pastor under the spiritual discipline of regular preparation is not happenstance; it is the natural result of the compassion and commitment of a faithful steward of the gospel.

Prepared and printed prayers need not exclude opportunity for personal intercession and petition from the pastor or from members of the congregation. A regularly included petition naming the sick of the congregation and providing opportunity for congregational members to add other names or concerns, either silently or aloud, can become an important weekly moment of corporate intercession. The form of the petition need be neither elaborate nor specific in terms of the nature of the illness or the need of the person. In other words, the petition should not reveal medical prognosis or embarrassing information, such as, "Lord, we pray for Mary Smith who found out this week she is going to die from breast cancer within six months" or "Lord, hear our prayer for John Jones, who is suffering these days from painful hemorrhoids." Rather, a petition like the following is more appropriate: "Let us pray for all who are sick in body, mind, or spirit and are in need of the healing presence of Christ. Especially today we pray for Mary Smith, John Jones, and (names). Lord, in your mercy, hear our prayer."

Such a format allows for personal intercession without inappropriate revelation. If people want to know more about Mary or John they can ask after the worship service. It also is best to obtain permission to use even the name of a person in public prayer. Do not assume that everyone wants such information publicly disclosed. As many as one in every eight to ten persons I ask tells me he or she would prefer not to be included in the spoken prayers, but rather silently from the altar. Often there are good reasons for this. Sometimes they aren't up to responding to questions, which might require painful or awkward answers, and sometimes they are suffering too much to be visited by well-intended friends. Remember too that silence about some things we know is a necessary discipline of the pastoral office we hold. It is part of our pastoral calling to carry in silence the burdens of others we would much prefer to deliver ourselves of.

Suggested Sabbath Bible Reading

The title of this book, *The Approaching Sabbath*, indicates that the pastor is in preparation each week for meeting the people of God on the Sabbath. No other task on that day of the Lord is more important than the proclamation of God's word. Many denominations, evangelical and Protestant, have agreed on a common set of texts for reading on the Sabbath, the lectionary. The lectionary is often intended as a focal point for the proclamation of the sermon. But it can also be used for formational purposes in the discipline of the pastor, as the Sabbath approaches.

The proposed Revised Common Lectionary is scheduled for official release in 1992. The readings for that edition are nearly set as of the first printing of this book. If any changes occur, the reader should not be dismayed with this edition but consider the intent of its listing in this book.* Along with chapter 5 on the discipline of reading the Bible for devotional purposes, we suggest that the Sunday lections can

---

*In some cases a reading from Acts is substituted for the Old Testament or Epistle. Numbers in brackets refer to Sundays in the Lutheran (ELCA) lectionary.

provide an outstanding list of Bible readings for spiritual reflection. Meditation on these texts will enliven preaching and deepen spiritual maturity regardless of whether you favor or oppose lectionary preaching.

If you wish to pursue a lectionary approach to all of your daily Bible reading, we suggest that you obtain a copy of the *Book of Common Prayer*. This approach has the advantage of a more consecutive reading through books of the Bible, with suggested lections for each day of the week. Regardless of the approach taken, the pastor cannot speak to and for the people of God unless the pastor is hearing and reading the word of God.

Year A

OT	Psalm	Epistle	Gospel	Sabbath
Is 2:1-5	Ps 122	Rom 13:11-14	Mt 24:36-44	Advent 1
Is 11:1-10	Ps 72:1-8	Rom 15:4-13	Mt 3:1-12	Advent 2
Is 35:1-10	Ps 146:5-10 Lk 1:46b-55	Jas 5:7-10	Mt 11:2-11	Advent 3
Is 7:10-16	Ps 80:1-7	Rom 1:1-7	Mt 1:18-25	Advent 4
Is 9:2-7	Ps 96	Tit 2:11-14	Lk 2:1-14 (15-20)	Christmas Day 1
Is 62:6-12	Ps 97	Tit 3:4-7	Lk 2:(1-7)8-20	Christmas Day 2
Is 52:7-10	Ps 98	Heb 1:1-12	Jn 1:1-14	Christmas Day 3
Is 63:7-9	Ps 111	Heb 2:10-18	Mt 2:13-23	Christmas 1
Num 6:22-27	Ps 8	Gal 4:4-7	Lk 2:15-21	Holy Name
Ec 3:1-13	Ps 8	Rev 21:1-6a	Mt 25:31-46	New Year
Jer 31:7-14	Ps 147:12-20	Eph 1:3-14	Jn 1:1-18	Christmas 2
Is 60:1-6	Ps 72:1-14	Eph 3:1-12	Mt 2:1-12	Epiphany 1
Is 42:1-9	Ps 29	Acts 10:34-43	Mt 3:13-17	Baptism of the Lord
Is 49:1-7	Ps 40:1-11	I Cor 1:1-9	Jn 1:29-42	Epiphany 2
Is 9:1-4	Ps 27:1-6	I Cor 1:10-18	Mt 4:12-23	Epiphany 3
Mic 6:1-8	Ps 37:1-11	I Cor 1:18-31	Mt 5:1-12	Epiphany 4
Is 58:1-9a	Ps 112:1-9 (10)	I Cor 2:1-12 (13-16)	Mt 5:13-16	Epiphany 5
Dt 30:15-20	Ps 119:1-8	I Cor 3:1-9	Mt 5:17-26	Epiphany 6
Is 49:8-16a	Ps 62:5-12	I Cor 3:10-11, 16-23	Mt 5:27-37	Epiphany 7
Lev 19:1-2, 9-18	Ps 119:33-40	I Cor 4:1-5	Mt 5:38-48	Epiphany 8

SUGGESTED READING APPENDIX I

Ex 24:12-18	Ps 99	II Pet 1:16-21	Mt 17:1-9	Epiphany Last-Transfig
Is 58:1-12	Ps 51:1-12	II Cor 5:20b–6:10	Mt 6:1-6, 16-21	Ash Wednesday
Gen 2:15-17, 3:1-7	Ps 130	Rom 5:12-19	Mt 4:1-11	Lent 1
Gen 12:1-4a	Ps 33:18-22	Rom 4:1-5, 13-17	Jn 3:1-17	Lent 2
Ex 17:1-7	Ps 95	Rom 5:1-11	Jn 4:5-42	Lent 3
I Sam 16:1-13	Ps 23	Eph 5:8-14	Jn 9:1-41	Lent 4
Ezek 37:1-14	Ps 116:1-9	Rom 8:6-11	Jn 11:1-45	Lent 5
Is 50:4-9a	Ps 31:9-16	Phil 2:5-11	Mt 26:14–27:66	Palm/Passion Sunday
Is 42:1-9	Ps 36:5-10	Heb 9:11-15	Jn 12:1-11	Monday in Holy Week
Is 49:1-6	Ps 71:1-16	I Cor 1:18-31	Jn 12:20-36	Tuesday in Holy Week
Is 50:4-9a	Ps 70	Heb 12:1-3	Jn 13:21-32	Wednesday in Holy Week
Ex 12:1-14	Ps 116:12-19	I Cor 11:23-26	Jn 13:1-17, 31b-35	Holy Thursday
Is 52:13–53:12	Ps 22	Heb 4:14-16, 5:7-9	Jn 18:1–19:42	Good Friday
Job 14:1-14	Ps 31:1-4, 15-16	I Pet 4:1-8	Mt 27:57-66	Holy Saturday
Gen 1:1–2:4a	Ps 33:1-11			Easter Vigil
Gen 7:1-5, 11-18; 8:6-18; 9:8-13				
Gen 22:1-18	Ps 46			
Ex 14:10-31; 15:20-21	Ps 16			
Ex 15:1b-6, 11-13, 17-18	Ps 42			
Is 55:1-11	Ps 143			
Is 12:2-6	Ps 98			
	Ps 114			
Ezek 36:24-28				
Ezek 37:1-14				
Zeph 3:14-20				
Jer 31:1-6	Ps 118:14-24	Col 3:1-4	Jn 20:1-18	Easter
Is 25:6-9	Ps 114	Acts 5:27-32	Lk 24:13-49	Easter Evening
Acts 2:14a, 22-32	Ps 16:5-11	I Pet 1:3-9	Jn 20:19-31	Easter 2
Acts 2:14a, 36-41	Ps 116:12-19	I Pet 1:17-23	Lk 24:13-35	Easter 3
Acts 2:42-47	Ps 23	I Pet 2:19-25	Jn 10:1-10	Easter 4
Acts 7:55-60	Ps 31:1-8	I Pet 2:2-10	Jn 14:1-14	Easter 5
Acts 17:22-31	Ps 66:8-20	I Pet 3:13-22	Jn 14:15-21	Easter 6
Acts 1:1-11	Ps 47	Eph 1:15-23	Lk 24:44-53	Ascension

Acts 1:6-14	Ps 68:1-10	I Pet 4:12-14; 5:6-11	Jn 17:1-11	Easter 7
Acts 2:1-21	Ps 104:24-34	I Cor 12:3b-13	Jn 20:19-23	Pentecost
Gen 1:1–2:4a	Ps 104:1-9	II Cor 13:3b-14	Mt 28:16-20	Trinity Sunday
Gen 6:9-22	Ps 46	Rom 1:16-17, 3:21-28 (29-31)	Mt 7:21-29	Proper 4 [9]
Gen 12:1-9	Ps 33:12-22	Rom 4:13-25	Mt 9:9-13, 18b-26	Proper 5 [10]
Gen 18:1-15 (21:1-7)	Ps 116:1-14	Rom 5:6-11	Mt 9:35–10:8 (9-23)	Proper 6 [11]
Gen 21:8-21	Ps 11	Rom 6:1b-11	Mt 10:24-33	Proper 7 [12]
Gen 22:1-18	Ps 13	Rom 6:12-23	Mt 10:34-42	Proper 8 [13]
Gen 24:1-4, 10-21, 58-67	Ps 45:10-17	Rom 7:15-25a	Mt 11:16-19, 25-30	Proper 9 [14]
Gen 25:19-34	Ps 46	Rom 8:1-11	Mt 13:1-9, 18-23	Proper 10 [15]
Gen 28:10-19a	Ps 91:1-11	Rom 8:12-25	Mt 13:24-30, 36-43	Proper 11 [16]
Gen 29:15-28	Ps 128	Rom 8:26-39	Mt 13:31-33, 44-52	Proper 12 [17]
Gen 32:22-32	Ps 17:1-7, 15	Rom 9:1-5	Mt 14:13-21	Proper 13 [18]
Gen 37:1-4, 12-36	Ps 105:1-6 (7-15) 16-22	Rom 10:5-15	Mt 14:22-33	Proper 14 [19]
Gen 45:1-15	Ps 133	Rom 11:1-2a, 29-32	Mt 15:(10-20) 21-28	Proper 15 [20]
Ex 1:8–2:10	Ps 124	Rom 12:1-8	Mt 16:13-20	Proper 16 [21]
Ex 3:1-15	Ps 105:1-6, 23-26	Rom 12:9-21	Mt 16:21-28	Proper 17 [22]
Ex 12:1-14	Ps 149	Rom 13:8-14	Mt 18:15-20	Proper 18 [23]
Ex 14:19-31	Ps 114	Rom 14:1-12	Mt 18:21-35	Proper 19 [24]
Ex 16:2-15	Ps 105:37-45	Phil 1:21-30	Mt 20:1-16	Proper 20 [25]
Ex 17:1-7	Ps 78:12-17, 38-39	Phil 2:1-13	Mt 21:23-32	Proper 21 [26]
Ex 20:1-20	Ps 19:7-14	Phil 3:4b-14	Mt 21:33-43	Proper 22 [27]
Ex 32:1-14	Ps 106:6-8, 19-23	Phil 4:1-9	Mt 22:1-14	Proper 23 [28]
Ex 33:12-23	Ps 99	I Thess 1:1-10	Mt 22:15-22	Proper 24 [29]
Jos 3:7-17	Ps 107:33-43	I Thess 2:1-8	Mt 22:34-46	Proper 25 [30]
Jg 4:1-7	Ps 123	I Thess 2:9-13	Mt 23:1-12	Proper 26 [31]
Rev 7:9-17	Ps 34:1-10	I Jn 3:1-3	Mt 5:1-12	All Saints
Jg 6:1-12	Ps 144	I Thess 4:13-18	Mt 25:1-13	Proper 27 [32]
Jg 16:23-31	Ps 36	I Thess 5:1-11	Mt 25:14-30	Proper 28 [33]
Ezek 34:11-16, 20-24	Ps 23	Eph 1:15-23	Mt 25:31-46	Reign of Christ [34]
Dt 8:7-18	Ps 65	II Cor 9:6-15	Lk 17:11-19	Thanksgiving

Year B

OT	Psalm	Epistle	Gospel	Sabbath
Is 64:1-9	Ps 80:1-7	I Cor 1:3-9	Mk 13:24-37	Advent 1
Is 40:1-11	Ps 85:8-13	II Pet 3:8-15a	Mk 1:1-8	Advent 2

105

Is 61:1-4, 8-11	Ps 126	I Thess 5:16-24	Jn 1:6-8, 19-28	Advent 3
II Sam 7:1-11, 16	Ps 89:1-4, 19-24	Rom 16:25-27	Lk 1:26-38	Advent 4
Is 9:2-7	Ps 96	Tit 2:11-14	Lk 2:1-14 (15-20)	Christmas Day 1
Is 62:6-12	Ps 97	Tit 3:4-7	Lk 2:(1-7)8-20	Christmas Day 2
Is 52:7-10	Ps 98	Heb 1:1-12	Jn 1:1-14	Christmas Day 3
Is 61:10–62:3	Ps 111	Gal 4:4-7	Lk 2:22-40	Christmas 1
Num 6:22-27	Ps 8	Phil 2:5-11	Lk 2:15-21	Holy Name
Ec 3:1-13	Ps 8	Rev 21:1-6a	Mt 25:31-46	New Year
Jer 31:7-14	Ps 147:12-20	Eph 1:3-14	Jn 1:1-18	Christmas 2
Is 60:1-6	Ps 72:1-14	Eph 3:1-12	Mt 2:1-12	Epiphany
Gen 1:1-5	Ps 29	Acts 19:1-7	Mk 1:4-11	Baptism of the Lord [1]
I Sam 3:1-10 (11-20)	Ps 139:7-18	I Cor 6:12-20	Jn 1:43-51	Epiphany 2
Jon 3:1-5, 10	Ps 62:5-12	I Cor 7:29-31	Mk 1:14-20	Epiphany 3
Dt 18:15-20	Ps 111	I Cor 8:1-13	Mk 1:21-28	Epiphany 4
I Kgs 17:17-24	Ps 147:1-11	I Cor 9:16-23	Mk 1:29-39	Epiphany 5
II Kgs 5:1-14	Ps 32	I Cor 9:24-27	Mk 1:40-45	Epiphany 6
Is 43:18-25	Ps 41	II Cor 1:18-22	Mk 2:1-12	Epiphany 7
Hos 2:14-20	Ps 103:1-13	II Cor 3:1-6	Mk 2:13-22	Epiphany 8
II Kgs 2:1-12	Ps 50:1-6	II Cor 4:3-6	Mk 9:2-9	Epiphany Last-Transfig
Jl 2:1-2, 12-17	Ps 51:1-12	II Cor 5:20b–6:10	Mt 6:1-6, 16-21	Ash Wednesday
Gen 9:8-17	Ps 25:1-10	I Pet 3:18-22	Mk 1:9-15	Lent 1
Gen 22:1-14	Ps 22:23-31	Rom 4:13-25	Mk 8:31-38	Lent 2
Ex 20:1-17	Ps 19:7-14	I Cor 1:18-25	Jn 2:13-22	Lent 3
Num 21:4-9	Ps 137:1-6	Eph 2:1-10	Jn 3:14-21	Lent 4
Jer 31:31-34	Ps 51:10-17	Heb 5:5-10	Jn 12:20-33	Lent 5
Is 50:4-9a	Ps 31:9-16	Phil 2:5-11	Mk 14:1–15:47	Palm/Passion Sunday
Is 42:1-9	Ps 36:5-10	Heb 9:11-15	Jn 12:1-11	Monday in Holy Week
Is 49:1-6	Ps 71:1-16	I Cor 1:18-31	Jn 12:20-36	Tuesday in Holy Week
Is 50:4-9a	Ps 70	Heb 12:1-3	Jn 13:21-32	Wednesday in Holy Week
Ex 12:1-14	Ps 116:12-19	I Cor 11:23-26	Jn 13:1-17, 31b-35	Holy Thursday
Is 52:13–53:12	Ps 22	Heb 10:16-25	Jn 18:1–19:42	Good Friday
Job 14:1-14	Ps 31:1-4, 15-16	I Pet 4:1-8	Jn 19:38-42	Holy Saturday
Gen 1:1–2:4a	Ps 33:1-11	Rom 6:3-11	Mk 16:1-8	Easter Vigil
Gen 7:1-5, 11-18; 8:6-18; 9:8-13	Ps 46			
Gen 22:1-18	Ps 16			

SUGGESTED READING APPENDIX I

Ex 14:10-31; 15:20-21	Ps 19			
Ex 15:1b-6, 11-13, 17-18	Ps 42			
Is 55:1-11	Ps 143			
Is 12:2-6	Ps 98			
Ezek 36:24-28	Ps 114			
Ezek 37:1-14				
Zeph 3:14-20				
Is 25:6-9	Ps 118:14-24	I Cor 15:1-11	Mk 16:1-8	Easter
Is 25:6-9	Ps 114	Acts 5:27-32	Lk 24:13-49	Easter Evening
Acts 4:32-35	Ps 133	I Jn 1:1–2:2	Jn 20:19-31	Easter 2
Acts 3:12-19	Ps 4	I Jn 3:1-7	Lk 24:36b-48	Easter 3
Acts 4:5-12	Ps 23	I Jn 3:16-24	Jn 10:11-18	Easter 4
Acts 8:26-40	Ps 22:25-31	I Jn 4:7-21	Jn 15:1-8	Easter 5
Acts 10:44-48	Ps 98	I Jn 5:1-6	Jn 15:9-17	Easter 6
Acts 1:1-11	Ps 47	Eph 1:15-23	Lk 24:44-53	Ascension
Acts 1:15-17, 21-26	Ps 1	I Jn 5:9-13	Jn 17:6-19	Easter 7
Ezek 37:1-14	Ps 104:24-34	Rom 8:22-27	Jn 15:26-27; 16:4b-15	Pentecost
Is 6:1-8	Ps 29	Rom 8:12-17	Jn 3:1-17	Trinity Sunday
I Sam 3:1-10 (11-20)	Ps 139:7-18	II Cor 4:5-12	Mk 2:23–3:6	Proper 4 [9]
I Sam 8:4-11 (12-15) 16-19 (11:15)	Ps 138	II Cor 4:13–5:1	Mk 3:20-35	Proper 5 [10]
I Sam 16:1-13	Ps 20	II Cor 5:6-10 (11-13) 14-17	Mk 4:26-34	Proper 6 [11]
I Sam 17:(1a, 4-11, 19-23), 32-49	Ps 144:1-10	II Cor 6:1-13	Mk 4:35-41	Proper 7 [12]
I Sam 18:1-5 (II Sam 1:17, 23-26)	Ps 130	II Cor 8:7-15	Mk 5:21-43	Proper 8 [13]
II Sam 5:1-5, 9-10	Ps 48	II Cor 12:2-10	Mk 6:1-13	Proper 9 [14]
II Sam 6:1-5, 12b-19	Ps 24	Eph 1:3-14	Mk 6:14-29	Proper 10 [15]
II Sam 7:1-17	Ps 89:20-37	Eph 2:11-22	Mk 6:30-44	Proper 11 [16]
II Sam 11:1-15	Ps 53	Eph 3:14-21	Jn 6:1-15 (16-21)	Proper 12 [17]
II Sam 11:26–12:13a	Ps 32	Eph 4:1-13 (14-16)	Jn 6:(16-23) 24-35	Proper 13 [18]
II Sam 18:5-9, 15, 31-33	Ps 62	Eph 4:25–5:2	Jn 6:35, 41-51	Proper 14 [19]
I Kgs 2:10-12; 3:3-14	Ps 111	Eph 5:15-20	Jn 6:51-58	Proper 15 [20]
I Kgs 8:1, 6, 10-11, 22-30, 41-43	Ps 122	Eph 6:10-20	Jn 6:56-69	Proper 16 [21]

S of S 2:8-13	Ps 45:1-2, 6-9	Jas 1:17-27	Mk 7:1-8, 14-15, 21-23	Proper 17 [22]
Pr 1:20-33	Ps 19:7-14	Jas 2:1-10 (11-13) 14-17	Mk 7:24-37	Proper 18 [23]
Pr 22:1-2, 8-9, 22-23	Ps 125	Jas 3:1-12	Mk 8:27-38	Proper 19 [24]
Pr 31:10-31	Ps 1	Jas 3:13–4:3, 7-8a	Mk 9:30-37	Proper 20 [25]
Est 7:1-6, 9-10	Ps 124	Jas 5:13-20	Mk 9:38-50	Proper 21 [26]
Job 1:1, 6-12 (13–2:10)	Ps 13	Heb 1:1-4; 2:9-11	Mk 10:2-16	Proper 22 [27]
Job 23:1-9, 16-17	Ps 22:1-15	Heb 4:12-16	Mk 10:17-31	Proper 23 [28]
Job 38:1-7 (34-41)	Ps 104:1-9	Heb 5:1-10	Mk 10:35-45	Proper 24 [29]
Job 42:1-6, 10-17	Ps 34:1-8	Heb 7:23-28	Mk 10:46-52	Proper 25 [30]
Ru 1:1-18	Ps 146	Heb 9:11-14	Mk 12:28-34	Proper 26 [31]
Is 25:6-9	Ps 1	Rev 21:1-6a	Jn 11:32-44	All Saints
Ru 3:1-5; 4:13-17	Ps 127	Heb 9:24-28	Mk 12:38-44	Proper 27 [32]
I Sam 1:4-20	I Sam 2:1-10	Heb 10:11-25	Mk 13:1-8	Proper 28 [33]
II Sam 23:1-7	Ps 95	Heb 12:1-2, 18-24	Jn 18:33-37	Reign of Christ [34]
Jl 2:21-27	Ps 126	I Tim 2:1-7	Mt 6:25-33	Thanksgiving

Year C

OT	Psalm	Epistle	Gospel	Sabbath
Jer 33:14-16	Ps 25:1-10	I Thess 3:9-13	Lk 21:25-36	Advent 1
Mal 3:1-4	Ps 126	Phil 1:3-11	Lk 3:1-6	Advent 2
Zeph 3:14-20	Is 12:2-6	Phil 4:4-7	Lk 3:7-18	Advent 3
Mic 5:2-4	Lk 1:46b-55	Heb 10:5-10	Lk 1:39-45 (46-55)	Advent 4
Is 9:2-7	Ps 96	Tit 2:11-14	Lk 2:1-14 (15-20)	Christmas Day 1
Is 62:6-12	Ps 97	Tit 3:4-7	Lk 2:(1-7) 8-20	Christmas Day 2
Is 52:7-10	Ps 98	Heb 1:1-12	Jn 1:1-14	Christmas Day 3
I Sam 2:18-20, 26	Ps 111	Col 3:12-17	Lk 2:41-52	Christmas 1
Num 6:22-27	Ps 8	Phil 2:5-11	Lk 2:15-21	Holy Name
Ec 3:1-13	Ps 8	Rev 21:1-6a	Mt 25:31-46	New Year
Jer 31:7-14	Ps 147:12-20	Eph 1:3-14	Jn 1:1-18	Christmas 2
Is 60:1-6	Ps 72:1-14	Eph 3:1-12	Mt 2:1-12	Epiphany
Is 42:1-9	Ps 29	Acts 8:14-17	Lk 3:15-17, 21-22	Baptism of the Lord [1]
Is 62:1-5	Ps 36:5-10	I Cor 12:1-11	Jn 2:1-11	Epiphany 2
Is 61:1-4	Ps 19:7-14	I Cor 12:12-31a	Lk 4:14-21	Epiphany 3

SUGGESTED READING APPENDIX I

Jer 1:4-10	Ps 71:1-6	I Cor 13:1-13	Lk 4:21-30	Epiphany 4
Is 6:1-8(9-13)	Ps 138	I Cor 15:1-11	Lk 5:1-11	Epiphany 5
Jer 17:5-10	Ps 1	I Cor 15:12-20	Lk 6:17-26	Epiphany 6
Gen 45:3-11, 15	Ps 37:1-11	I Cor 15:35-38, 42-50	Lk 6:27-38	Epiphany 7
Is 55:10-13	Ps 92:1-4, 12-15	I Cor 15:51-58	Lk 6:39-49	Epiphany 8
Ex 34:29-35	Ps 99	II Cor 3:12–4:2	Lk 9:28-36	Epiphany Last-Transfig
Jl 2:1-2, 12-17	Ps 51:1-12	II Cor 5:20b–6:10	Mt 6:1-6, 16-21	Ash Wednesday
Dt 26:1-11	Ps 91:9-16	Rom 10:8b-13	Lk 4:1-13	Lent 1
Gen 15:1-12, 17-18	Ps 127	Phil 3:17–4:1	Lk 13:31-35	Lent 2
Ex 3:1-15	Ps 103:1-13	I Cor 10:1-13	Lk 13:1-9	Lent 3
Jos 5:9-12	Ps 34:1-8	II Cor 5:16-21	Lk 15:1-3, 11b-32	Lent 4
Is 43:16-21	Ps 126	Phil 3:8-14	Jn 12:1-8	Lent 5
Is 50:4-9a	Ps 31:9-16	Phil 2:5-11	Lk 22:14–23:56	Palm/Passion Sunday
Is 42:1-9	Ps 36:5-10	Heb 9:11-15	Jn 12:1-11	Monday in Holy Week
Is 49:1-6	Ps 71:1-16	I Cor 1:18-31	Jn 12:20-36	Tuesday in Holy Week
Is 50:4-9a	Ps 70	Heb 12:1-3	Jn 13:21-32	Wednesday in Holy Week
Ex 12:1-14	Ps 116:12-19	I Cor 11:23-26	Jn 13:1-17, 31b-35	Holy Thursday
Is 52:13–53:12	Ps 22	Heb 10:16-25	Jn 18:1–19:42	Good Friday
Job 14:1-14	Ps 31:1-4, 15-16	I Pet 4:1-8	Mt 27:57-66	Holy Saturday
Gen 1:1–2:4a	Ps 33:1-11	Rom 6:3-11	Lk 24:1-12	Easter Vigil
Gen 7:1-5, 11-18; 8:6-18; 9:8-13	Ps 46			
Gen 22:1-18	Ps 16			
Ex 14:10-31; 15:20-21	Ps 19			
Ex 15:1b-6, 11-13, 17-18	Ps 42			
Is 55:1-11	Ps 143			
Is 12:2-6	Ps 98			
	Ps 114			
Ezek 37:24-28				
Ezek 37:1-14				
Zeph 3:14-20				
Is 65:17-25	Ps 118:14-24	I Cor 15:19-26	Jn 20:1-18	Easter
Is 25:6-9	Ps 114	Acts 5:27-32	Lk 24:13-49	Easter Evening
Acts 5:27-32	Ps 118:14-29	Rev 1:4-8	Jn 20:19-31	Easter 2

Acts 9:1-6 (7-20)	Ps 30:4-12	Rev 5:11-14	Jn 21:1-19	Easter 3
Acts 13:13-16, 26-33	Ps 2	Rev 7:9-17	Jn 10:23-30	Easter 4
Acts 15:1-2, 22-29	Ps 24:1-6	Rev 21:1-6	Jn 13:31-35	Easter 5
Acts 16:9-15	Ps 67	Rev 21:10, 22-27	Jn 14:23-29	Easter 6
Acts 1:1-11	Ps 47	Eph 1:15-23	Lk 24:44-53	Ascension
Acts 16:16-34	Ps 97	Rev 22:12-14, 16-17, 20-21	Jn 17:20-26	Easter 7
Gen 11:1-9	Ps 104:24-34	Rom 8:14-17	Jn 14:8-17, 25-27	Pentecost
Pr 8:1-4, 22-31	Ps 8	Rom 5:1-5	Jn 16:12-15	Trinity Sunday
I Kgs 21:1-10 (11-14) 15-20	Ps 5	Gal 1:1-12	Lk 7:1-10	Proper 4 [9]
I Kgs 17:8-16 (17-24)	Ps 146	Gal 1:11-24	Lk 7:11-17	Proper 5 [10]
I Kgs 18:20-21 (22-29) 30-39	Ps 145	Gal 2:20-39	Lk 7:36-50	Proper 6 [11]
I Kgs 19:1-4 (5-7) 8-15a	Ps 42	Gal 3:23-29	Lk 8:26-39	Proper 7 [12]
II Kgs 2:1-2, 6-14	Ps 77:1-2, 11-20	Gal 5:1, 13-25	Lk 9:51-62	Proper 8 [13]
II Kgs 5:1-15a	Ps 30	Gal 6:1-16	Lk 10:1-11, 16-20	Proper 9 [14]
Am 1:1; 7:7-17	Ps 82	Col 1:1-14	Lk 10:25-37	Proper 10 [15]
Am 8:1-12	Ps 52	Col 1:15-29	Lk 10:38-42	Proper 11 [16]
Hos 1:1-10	Ps 85	Col 2:6-15	Lk 11:1-13	Proper 12 [17]
Hos 11:1-11	Ps 107:1-9	Col 3:1-11	Lk 12:13-21	Proper 13 [18]
Is 1:1, 10-20	Ps 50:1-8 22-23	Heb 11:1-3, 8-19	Lk 12:32-40	Proper 14 [19]
Is 5:1-7	Ps 80:1-2, 8-19	Heb 12:1-2	Lk 12:49-56	Proper 15 [20]
Jer 1:4-10	Ps 71:1-6	Heb 12:18-29	Lk 13:10-17	Proper 16 [21]
Jer 2:4-13	Ps 78:1-4, 9-16	Heb 13:1-8	Lk 14:1, 7-14	Proper 17 [22]
Jer 18:1-11	Ps 139:1-6, 13-18	Philem 1-21	Lk 14:25-33	Proper 18 [23]
Jer 4:11-12, 22-28	Ps 53	I Tim 1:12-17	Lk 15:1-10	Proper 19 [24]
Num 21:4b-9	Ps 78:1-2, 34-38	I Cor 1:18-24	Jn 3:13-17	Holy Cross
Jer 8:18–9:1	Ps 79:1-9	I Tim 2:1-7	Lk 16:1-13	Proper 20 [25]
Jer 32:1-3, 6-15	Ps 85	I Tim 6:6-19	Lk 16:19-31	Proper 21 [26]
Lam 1:1-6	Ps 74	II Tim 1:1-14	Lk 17:5-10	Proper 22 [27]
Jer 29:1, 4-7	Ps 66:1-12	II Tim 2:8-15	Lk 17:11-19	Proper 23 [28]
Jer 31:27-34	Ps 119:65-71	II Tim 3:14–4:5	Lk 18:1-8	Proper 24 [29]
Jl 2:23-32a	Ps 107:1-3, 33-43	II Tim 4:6-8, 16-18	Lk 18:9-14	Proper 25 [30]

SUGGESTED READING APPENDIX I

Hab 1:1-4; 2:1-4	Ps 119:137-44	II Thess 1:1-4, 11-12	Lk 19:1-10	Proper 26 [31]
Dan 7:1-3, 15-18	Ps 149	Eph 1:11-23	Lk 6:20-36	All Saints
Hag 1:15b-2:9	Ps 65:1-13	II Thess 2:13-3:5	Lk 20:27-38	Proper 27 [32]
Is 65:17-25	Ps 12	II Thess 3:6-13	Lk 21:5-19	Proper 28 [33]
Jer 23:1-6	Lk 1:68-79	Col 1:11-20	Lk 23:33-43	Reign of Christ [34]
Dt 26:1-11	Ps 100	Phil 4:4-9	Jn 6:25-35	Thanksgiving

Suggested Reading

The suggestions presented here are divided into two principal categories: Fiction and Nonfiction. Each principal category is subdivided into three smaller categories. These subcategories are Classic Literature, Late-twentieth-century Works, and Short Stories under Fiction; and Biography and Autobiography, Cultural Currents and Analyses, and Essayists and Wordsmiths under Nonfiction. Examples of books in each subcategory are presented with brief annotations. These suggestions are intended as a reading list for spiritual discipline. Actual individual choices for reading will vary depending on the interests and needs of the reader. The goal is to develop balance in choosing reading material and to compile categories from which to choose reading material that helps form and maintain such balance.

I. Fiction

  A) Classic Literature

    1) **The Brothers Karamazov,** Fyodor Dostoevski.

Central themes in this novel include a psychological obsession, a sordid love triangle, a gripping courtroom drama, and the underlying tension of the search for truth about humankind, life, and the existence and purposes of God.

2) **Crime and Punishment,** Fyodor Dostoevski. This novel is an unsurpassed study of pride, rebellion, and guilt. It is filled with profound images of human struggle and suffering and the need for redemption and resurrection.

3) **Jude the Obscure,** Thomas Hardy. This novel offers a penetrating psychological look into the life of an impoverished stone mason who aspires to the ministry.

4) **Tess of the D'Urbervilles**, Thomas Hardy. Although this novel offers an indictment of Victorian society, it describes the annihilation of innocence, which remains a timely theme today.

B) Late-twentieth-century Works

1) *Regional*
   (a) **The Second Coming,** Walker Percy.
   (b) **Ironweed,** William Kennedy.
   What is gained in reading the novels of regional writers is clarity about the influences that form the thought patterns and values of a particular people. Percy's region is the American South. Kennedy's is Albany, New York.

2) *Women's Perspective*
   (a) **The Company of Women,** Mary Gordon.

(b) **Final Payments,** Mary Gordon.

These novels deal with basic human concerns like love, hate, loyalty, guilt, dependency, and faith from a woman's perspective and the point of view of female characters.

3) *Fantasy and Mystery*
  (a) **The Depforth Trilogy** *(Fifth Business, The Manticore,* and *World of Wonders),* Robertson Davies.
  (b) **The Book of the Dun Cow,** and **The Book of Sorrows,** Walter Wangerin.
  (c) **The Name of the Rose,** Umberto Eco.

Reading novels of fantasy and mystery can feed the imagination and nurture a sense of wonder and of the holy in the reader. They often center on the universal struggle between good and evil and are filled with elements of the mystical, with wonder and the darker currents of ambition and vengeance, and with archetypal images of love and death.

4) *Jewish Life and Faith*
  (a) **Night, The Accident,** Elie Wiesel.
  (b) **The Chosen, The Promise, Davita's Harp,** Chaim Potok.

Of the world's many cultures and religions it seems especially important that a pastor should be knowledgeable about Judaism and its people. These novels speak powerfully of the suffering, tragedy, complexity, and heroic struggle of a people who have seen and experienced much evil, and whose memory of it, though a necessary burden, is hard to bear.

5) *Christian Life and Faith*
   (a) **The Irrational Season, Walking on Water,** Madeleine L'Engle.
   (b) **Whistling in the Dark: An ABC Theologized,** Frederick Buechner.
   (c) **The Mystery of the Word: Parables of Everyday Faith,** Mike Mason.
   (d) **Morte D'Urban,** J. F. Powers.
   There are many insightful and sensitive books written about Christian life and faith. These represent some of the richness of the variety available. L'Engle's essays employ the insights of an artist in understanding the deepest implications of our life as children of God. Buechner's book reveals the divine mystery present in ordinary words and everyday experiences. Mason's writing focuses on the stories of men and women who are struggling to live the gospel daily. Powers' novel is an excellent treatment of ambition among clergy.

6) *Religious Themes*
   (a) **The Power and the Glory,** Graham Greene.
   (b) **The Final Beast, Godric,** Frederick Buechner.
   Although much good fiction deals with issues that touch on human relationship to the transcendent, the books of certain writers such as these, do so more intentionally than others. Greene's whiskey priest offers a modern crucifixion story of faith struggling with limitation,

doubt, and fear. Buechner's character, Godric, is a twelfth-century English holy man whose life explores the nature of spirituality from an earthy, honest point of view.

7) *Children's Literature*
   (a) **Charlotte's Web,** E. B. White.
   (b) **A Wrinkle in Time,** Madeleine L'Engle. This category is included because it is frequently overlooked and underestimated by adults. Children's books have a sense of simplicity, clarity, wonder, and respect for words, people, animals, and objects. To read good children's literature keeps the adult in touch with children and with the child in himself. Many adults could benefit by nurturing a healthy child in themselves with the capacity for wonder, humor, resiliency, and living fully in the present moment the way that children do.

8) *Literature from Other Cultures*
   (a) **Silence, The Samurai,** Shusaku Endo.
   (b) **One Hundred Years of Solitude,** Gabriel Garcia Marquez.
   (c) **Cry the Beloved Country,** Alan Paton. Reading novels from other cultures broadens understanding and deepens identification with people who may speak a different language and have different customs yet share much that is human in common. There are tears and longing and love and death in every culture. Great literature from around the world helps keep the remembrance of

this human connection alive. Willa
Cather was right. There are only two or
three human stories, but they are often
repeated.

C) Short Stories

1) *American Cultural Stories*
   (a) **The Stories of John Cheever,** John
       Cheever.
   (b) **Short Shorts: An Anthology of the
       Shortest Stories,** ed. Irving and Glana
       Howe.
   (c) **The Best American Short Stories of
       1984,** ed. John Updike, with Shannon
       Ravenel. Writers like John Cheever pres-
       ent powerful and concisely written ac-
       counts of the sometimes hateful, often
       melancholy and confused lives of many
       Americans. *Short Shorts* presents excel-
       lent examples of clarity and restraint in
       the development of lucid images and
       ideas. *The Best American Short Stories*
       has been published annually since 1934.
       Each new annual edition is a good source
       of the best currently published American
       short stories. The reader who is particu-
       larly interested in the development of
       story literature and in a good bibliogra-
       phy on storytelling and tales is referred
       to Ruth Sawyer's book *The Way of the
       Storyteller* (Penguin Books, 1982).

2) *Jewish Tales and Stories*
   (a) **Tales of the Hasidim,** Martin Buber.

(b) **Hasidic Tales of the Holocaust,** Yoffa Eliach.

(c) **Four Hasidic Masters and Their Struggle Against Melancholy,** Elie Wiesel.

(d) **A Young Man in Search of Love, Reaches of Heaven: A Story of the Baal Shem Tov,** Isaac Bashevis Singer.

The stories of Jewish writers are often filled with the full range of human experience from profound suffering to profound joy. Buber's two-volume collection is filled with penetrating, thought-provoking tales of the lives of the early and late-eighteenth-century members of the eastern European Hasidic movement, most notably tales centering on the founder of the movement, the Baal Shem Tov. Eliach's contribution is twofold: She presents the first original Hasidic tales in a century and she intentionally includes the stories of Hasidic women in her collection. Wiesel's stories describe the spiritual ecstasy, existential melancholy and loneliness that often accompanies vision and greatness. The excellent writing of Isaac Bashevis Singer is a model of clarity and simplicity.

3) *Regional Storytellers*

(a) **The Complete Stories of Flannery O'Connor,** Flannery O'Connor.

(b) **Happy to Be Here, Lake Wobegon Days,** Garrison Keillor.

O'Connor's stories deal with universal themes of suffering and evil as experienced by complex and believable characters from the American South. Thomas Merton once said of her that he wrote her name with honor, for all the truth and all the craft with which she shows man's fall and dishonor. Keillor's stories are of life in the upper Midwest. They are at the same time serious and humorous, filled with insight into the folkways and values of small-town people in America's heartland.

4) *Anthologies of Stories for Children and Adults*
   (a) **Along the Water's Edge,** Daniel Juniper.
   (b) **Speaking in Stories, Stories for Telling, Stories for the Journey,** William White.
   (c) **Story Sunday, Gathered Round,** John Aurelio.
   (d) **Friends for Life,** Michael Williams.
   (e) **The Way of the Wolf, Nenshu and the Tiger,** Martin Bell.
   Juniper's collection is keyed to the use of stories with the lectionary and church year. White's *Speaking in Stories* has a good bibliography of books of stories. Aurelio's stories contain scriptural and doctrinal themes appropriate for use in preaching, teaching, and counseling ministries. Williams' book is intended for use in worship settings. Bell's stories present the gospel in compelling and creative new ways.

II. Nonfiction

A) Biography and Autobiography

1) *Writers*
   (a) **Growing Up,** Russell Baker.
   (b) **One Writer's Beginnings,** Eudora Welty.
   (c) **A Young Man in Search of Love,** Isaac Bashevis Singer.
   Writers' autobiographies often depict the central role of memory in bringing meaning and confluence to individual lives. Such literary autobiographies can help pastors see and remember that evoking memories is a powerful and potentially healing resource for oneself and for others.

2) *Famous Preachers*
   (a) **Leslie Weatherhead: A Personal Portrait,** A. Kingsley Weatherhead.
   (b) **One Man's Way,** Arthur Gordon.
   (c) **This Grace Given, Grace Thus Far,** David H. Read.
   Biographies such as these point out that there is struggle, disappointment, and opposition in every life and that people of great ability often have more of such things than most people do. Popular though Leslie Weatherhead was, for instance, often more than half of the hundreds of letters he received in response to a broadcast sermon were firmly opposed, even hostile, to his views. Arthur Gordon's biography of Norman Vincent Peale details how the life of any one human being is much too complex and diverse to be limited only to certain stereotypical understandings, such as "positive thinking" in Peale's

case. David H. C. Read's two-part autobiography encourages those who read it
to more informed and careful reflection
upon their own lives and upon the people
and events that have formed their character and shaped the direction their lives
have taken.

3) *Spiritual Autobiography*
   (a) **The Seven Storey Mountain,** Thomas
   Merton.
   (b) **The Sacred Journey, Now and Then,**
   Frederick Buechner.
   Autobiographies such as these are filled
   with spiritual insight and sensitivity to
   experience that allows no deceit and is
   often painful in its honesty. They share
   an underlying motif: Every moment of
   life is a bearer of the holy, a sacred
   moment pregnant with meaning. Such
   writers nurture in others an awareness
   of the presence of the holy in the
   ordinary and of the sacredness of people
   and events that make up the moments
   and days of a lifetime.

4) *Regional and Cultural Biographies*
   (a) **Brother to a Dragonfly,** Will Campbell.
   (b) **Will Campbell and the Soul of the
   South,** Thomas L. Connelly.
   Biographies such as these, one by Will
   Campbell about his brother and the
   other about Campbell himself, help
   readers visualize experiences and
   images in the lives of real people.
   Visualizing specific experiences under-

scores the principle that the universal is best understood and responded to by looking at a particular instance of it, whether that universal be love or longing or hate or fear or death.

5) *Great Figures of Church and State*
   (a) **Thomas More,** R. W. Chambers.
   (b) **Confessions,** Augustine.
   (c) **Here I Stand: A Life of Martin Luther,** Roland Bainton.
   (d) **John Wesley,** Stanley Ayling.
   The reason for including this as a category is that the great people of a given time are often closely identified with and had influence on the great issues of their time. This was true, for instance, of Thomas More's great struggle with Henry VIII over the divorce of Catherine and the supremacy of the king over the church. It was also true of Augustine and of others who have had great influence on church and state, for example, Martin Luther, John Calvin, John Wesley, Jonathan Edwards, and Martin Luther King, Jr.

B) Cultural Currents and Analyses

   1) *Cultural Critique*

      (a) **The Culture of Narcissism,** Christopher Lasch.
      (b) **Habits of the Heart: Individualism and Commitment in American Life,** Robert Bellah.

(c) **Amusing Ourselves to Death: Public Discourse in the Age of Show Business,** Neil Postman.

This category covers a broad range, but it is not an attempt to know something about all the cross currents of today's culture. Rather what is sought is a reasonably good general knowledge of those broad influences upon culture which assume a wide variety of expression in art, music, theater, literature, and various media forms. By reading recognized books of cultural analysis and current sociological studies, pastors can keep abreast of these cultural influences and have at hand tools to help interpret them. For instance, Lasch's book offers a critical and penetrating perspective on the narcissistic personality of our time. Bellah's study is based on interviews with two hundred white, middle-class Americans responding to such basic questions as "How ought we to live?" and "What is our character?" Postman's book is a commentary on the negative influence of television entertainment on the American people.

2) *Professional Journals and Magazines*
   (a) **The Christian Century, Sojourners.**
   (b) **Harper's, The Atlantic.**
   (c) **Time, Newsweek.**

The selection of journals and magazines is a highly individual choice. The intent here is to highlight their use as current and concise communicators and interpreters of cultural trends and analysis. Editorial, feature, book review, and reader response sections of most leading journals and magazines offer weekly or monthly up-to-date perspectives on current events, trends, and new books.

C) Essayists and Wordsmiths

1) *Art and Nature*
   (a) **Walking on Water, The Irrational Season,** Madeleine L'Engle.
   (b) **Pilgrim at Tinker Creek, Holy the Firm,** Annie Dillard.
   (c) **Pastorale—A Natural History of Sorts,** Jake Page.
   Essayists and wordsmiths provide disciplined models in the use of the English language and clear, provocative comment on many areas of human thought and activity. For example, L'Engle deals with such themes as cosmos and chaos, time, journey, and silence in her essays. Annie Dillard's contribution lies in her power of detailed description, which is at times harsh but is always clear and never less than a longing search for the holy in the common. Page's essays on nature blend wit and humor with serious reflection, modeling clarity of thought and sensitivity to the extraordinary in the ordinary.

2) *Religion and Culture*
   (a) **Grace Notes and Other Fragments, Gravity and Grace: Reflections and Provocations,** Joseph Sittler.

(b) **Leaves from the Notebook of a Tamed Cynic,** Reinhold Niebuhr.

(c) **A Room Called Remember,** Frederick Buechner.

Themes from essayists such as these include serious, humorous, informed reflection on topics such as faith, ministry, theology, education, language, modern culture, aging, and moral discourse in a nuclear age. Reading the essays of such seminal religious writers as these can add depth to a pastor's own reflection on life and ministry.

3) *Language and Ideas*

(a) **Letters of E. B. White, Essays of E. B. White,** E. B. White.

(b) **Habitations of the Word,** William H. Gass.

The writing of E. B. White sets the standard of excellence in matters of style, grace, and simplicity in the presentation of ideas. It has been said of him that if we are remembered as a civilized era it will be in part because the historians of the future will decide that a writer of such grace and control could not have been produced by a generation wholly lacking in such qualities. Other essayists, such as William H. Gass, underscore the importance of words as symbols and means of communicating to others. Evidence of the importance of words is found in his essay entitled "And," which is an informative twenty-five-page analysis of the single word *and*.

Notes

Chapter 1: The Spiritual Formation of the Pastor

1. Dag Hammarskjöld, *Markings* (New York: Ballantine Books, 1983), p. 12.
2. M. Robert Mulholland, Jr., *Shaped by the Word: The Power of Scripture in Spiritual Formation* (Nashville: The Upper Room, 1985), p. 28.
3. Margaret Fletcher Clark, "Ten Models of Ordained Ministry," *Action Information* (November-December 1983), pp. 1-4.
4. Lyle E. Schaller, *The Pastor and the People: Building a New Partnership for Effective Ministry* (Nashville: Abingdon Press, 1973), p. 46.
5. John C. Wagner, "Spirituality and Administration: The Sign of Integrity," *Weavings* (July-August 1988), pp. 15-26.
6. William Willimon and Stanley Hauerwas, "Limits of Care," *Word and World* (Summer 1990), p. 251.
7. Thomas R. Kelly, *A Testament of Devotion* (New York: Harper & Row, Publishers, 1941), p. 114.
8. Ibid.
9. Gardner Taylor, "The Most in the Least," The Academy of Preachers Lectures, Lutheran Theological Seminary at Philadelphia, June 24, 1986.
10. Joseph Sittler, *Gravity and Grace: Reflections and Provocations* (Minneapolis: Augsburg Publishing House, 1986), p. 49.

NOTES

Chapter 2: Spiritual Formation in the Family

1. J. C. Wynn, "The Hole in Our Holiness Is Other People," *Spiritual Life* (Fall 1989), p. 164.
2. A version of this section was first published in the June 3, 1987, issue of *The Lutheran*, copyright © 1987. Reprinted by permission of Augsburg Fortress.

Chapter 3: The Study of Life as Spiritual Formation

1. George Sweazy, *Preaching the Good News* (Englewood Cliffs, N.J.: Prentice-Hall, 1976), p. 105.
2. Annie Dillard, *Holy the Firm* (New York: Harper Colophon Books, 1977), pp. 16-18.
3. Sittler, *Gravity and Grace*, p. 54.
4. Anne Morrow Lindbergh, *Gift from the Sea* (New York: Vintage Books, 1978), p. 9.
5. Ernest Campbell, "Who Is on the Lord's Side?" The Academy of Preachers Lectures, Lutheran Theological Seminary at Philadelphia, June 24, 1986.
6. Donald Nicholl, *Holiness* (New York: Seabury Press, 1983), p. 16.
7. J. Barrie Shepherd, "Chimney Cleaning," used by permission of the author.
8. Ira Progoff, *At a Journal Workshop* (New York: Dialogue House, 1975).

Chapter 4: Prayer as Spiritual Formation

1. Doberstein, *Minister's Prayer Book*, pp. 279-80.
2. Ibid., p. 304.

Chapter 5: Reading the Bible

1. Thomas S. Kepler, *The Table Talk of Martin Luther* (Grand Rapids, Mich.: Baker Book House, 1983), p. 6.
2. Sittler, *Gravity and Grace*, pp. 34-35.
3. Robert Mulholland, "Spiritual Reading of Scripture," *Weavings* (November-December 1988), pp. 26-32.

Chapter 6: Reading as Spiritual Formation

1. Quoted in John W. Doberstein, *Minister's Prayer Book* (Philadelphia: Fortress Press, 1959), p. 311.

NOTES

2. Fred B. Craddock, "Preaching as Story-telling," Lecture tape, (Atlanta: PRTVC Audio Cassettes, 1980).
3. Gustave Flaubert, *Madame Bovary* (New York: Simon and Schuster, 1943), p. 331.
4. Garrison Keillor, *Lake Wobegon Days* (New York: Viking Penguin, 1985), p. 334.
5. Richard J. Foster, *Celebration of Discipline: The Path to Spiritual Growth* (New York: Harper & Row, Publishers, 1978), p. 56.

Chapter 7: Corporate Devotional Life

1. Larry McMurtry, *Lonesome Dove* (New York: Pocket Books, 1985), p. 235.
2. Doberstein, *Minister's Prayer Book*, p. 130.